Levinas beyond the
Horizons of Cartesianism

American University Studies

Series V
Philosophy
Vol. 150

PETER LANG
New York • Washington, D.C./Baltimore • San Francisco
Bern • Frankfurt am Main • Berlin • Vienna • Paris

Anthony F. Beavers

Levinas beyond the Horizons of Cartesianism

An Inquiry into the Metaphysics of Morals

PETER LANG
New York • Washington, D.C./Baltimore • San Francisco
Bern • Frankfurt am Main • Berlin • Vienna • Paris

Library of Congress Cataloging-in-Publication Data

Beavers, Anthony F. (Anthony Francis).
 Levinas beyond the horizons of Cartesianism: an inquiry into the
 metaphysics of morals / Anthony F. Beavers.
    p.   cm. — (American university studies. Series V, Philosophy;
 vol. 150)
    Includes bibliographical references.
    1. Ethics. 2. Lévinas, Emmanuel—Ethics. 3. Other minds (Theory of
 knowledge) I. Title. II. Series.
 BJ1031.B438   171'.2—dc20   93-35785
 ISBN 0-8204-2173-1
 ISSN 0739-6392

Die Deutsche Bibliothek-CIP-Einheitsaufnahme

Beavers, Anthony F.:
Levinas beyond the horizons of Cartesianism: an inquiry into the metaphysics
of morals / Anthony F. Beavers. - New York; San Francisco; Bern;
Washington, D.C./Baltimore; Frankfurt am Main; Berlin; Wien; Paris: Lang.
 (American university studies: Ser. 5, Philosophy; Vol. 150)
 ISBN 0-8204-2173-1
NE: American university studies / 05

© 1995 Peter Lang Publishing, Inc., New York

For my wife, Julia

Contents

Introduction

This book presents Emmanuel Levinas' central insights from the perspective of Descartes' thought. I have chosen to adopt this approach because the single most important characteristic of Levinas' work is the quest for exteriority, for otherness. Since this quest is first articulated by Descartes, it seems fitting to begin here and explain precisely why it has a legitimate place in philosophical inquiry. I begin Chapter One considering Descartes' reduction of experience to the mind, to what the tradition will later call "rational subjectivity." I then show how subjectivity is clarified by Kant and Husserl. Kant demonstrates that Descartes' concern over the existence of things outside the self is not a pressing philosophical issue; that question belongs to "speculative metaphysics." More importantly, he shows that answering the question is unnecessary, since knowledge can be explained solely in terms of objects *as they appear within human experience*. Their status as "things-in-themselves" need not and cannot be guaranteed.

Taking Kant seriously, Husserl invents the phenomenological method. This method attempts to explain consciousness by redefining the world in terms of experience only. If the world unfolds in terms of experience, then it unfolds only in *my* experience; Husserl's method entails redefining the world strictly in terms of the self. That Husserl can explain consciousness without recourse to the other means, for Levinas, as it does for Heidegger, that apparently the type of consciousness that Husserl describes—representational or rational consciousness—is, in fact, solipsistic. Levinas writes, "The most audacious and remote knowledge does not put us in communion with the truly other; it does not take the place of sociality; it is still and always a solitude."[1]

Heidegger sets out to solve the problem of solipsism by showing that knowledge does not unfold in isolation from lived experience and that Husserl's method rests on the implicit assumption that it does. Heidegger attempts to ground knowledge existentially by describing it as one of the many modes of human being. Prior to knowing, the human is already in-the-world.

Thus, it is a "scandal of philosophy" that anyone would question this world's existence; it is given in the human being's creative activity. This being dwells in-the-world and is connected to everything else by way of functions. He is a builder, the world is his workshop, and the implements with which he builds things are his tools. Together they form a referential totality. But, while this totality surpasses the limits of rational subjectivity, it does not surpass consciousness. Levinas implies that Heidegger's "world" is also constructed by a builder, who adjusts and readjusts references into a coherent worldview, partially at the hands of others, who are not, therefore, situated within that world. There are, in other words, levels of consciousness more primordial than the level of function.

Levinas points to one of these to show that if human beings do dwell with real, concrete others, contact between the self and other cannot occur in reason or in function, but in affectivity, which is intimately tied to sensibility. In taking this route to the "lower" levels of consciousness, Levinas is actually repeating a Cartesian theme. Even though he departs from the tradition of rational subjectivity that began with Descartes and was clarified by Kant, Husserl and Heidegger, even though he departs from mainstream Cartesianism, he is still within the grip of Descartes' philosophy. In fact, Levinas shares a kinship with Descartes that Kant, Husserl, and Heidegger do not share. This kinship unfolds on two levels. One is the level of the finite mind turned inside out by the idea of infinity. Descartes' realization that the idea of the infinite could not be created by a finite mind and that it, therefore, must have been put into this mind by the infinite itself indicates, for Levinas, a breach of totality, a rupture of the world that signals the presence of the other. Since this moment provides the contact with the other that animates so much of Levinas' work, one scholar notes that Descartes provides Levinas with "the epistemological keynote to his entire theory."[2]

In addition, Levinas shares Descartes' characterization of sensibility as an irrational, yet necessary, component of human experience. On the level of sense, the mind is incarnate in the body and exposed to exteriority. But, since Descartes' thought has been handed down to us primarily in the tradition of rational subjectivity, his thoughts on mind-body unity and sensibility have largely been ignored. So, I dedicate all of Chapter Two to these themes. However, since sensibility and all that it entails is not usually included in an exposition of Descartes, this chapter may sound surprisingly un-Cartesian, thereby making it necessary to develop many themes that will not be tied to Levinas explicitly. I include these because readers have not been disposed to accept my reading of Descartes without them.

Descartes characterizes knowing as a departure from sensibility, an act of "withdrawing the mind from the senses." He assigns the passions to this level of life, noting that in passion the human being is defined by receptivity as opposed to the activity of thinking. Later in Chapter Three, Levinas will characterize this sensual life as enjoyment and possession, preserving its receptive character. Chapter Two ends by examining the transition from passion to morals in Descartes' thought. Since morality is a matter of governing practical life, it is also relegated to the level of life as it is lived. Consequently, the passions have an important role in explaining and developing morality. Moral life, for Descartes, is a matter of properly using the will to control the passions. This control results in a completely integrated human being, a mind-body unity, manifested in Descartes' work by an existential connection between self-esteem and generosity.

The remaining chapters of this book clarify the themes of Chapter Two by presenting Levinas' descriptions of the terrain unearthed by Descartes. In Chapter Three, Levinas' thought is situated within Cartesian structures. Here, I discuss his thoughts on sensibility, enjoyment, incarnate consciousness, affective intentionality, etc., in light of the problematic indicated in Chapter One, the quest for exteriority. Life as it is lived is a matter of possession, of absorbing the exterior into the self under the rubric of enjoyment. Since in enjoyment exteriority is consumed, sensual life does not yet permit a stable relationship with what is other; in sensuality, the self possesses the other, and therefore, denies its character as other.

This process of possession changes when I encounter the face of the other person in my experience. The other, as revealed in the face-to-face, questions my egoist possession of the world. My desire to possess the other bears witness to the other's presence; that the other resists my possession bears witness to the very otherness of the other, her transcendence. She is always unknown and infinite, the stranger. She can neither be absorbed into the intellect, reduced to the thought that defines my subjectivity, nor consumed by my sensuous enjoyment. Chapter Three ends with an examination of the other's intrusion into my project of living thereby forcing me momentarily to stop this project to take her into account. Here, ethics are born precisely as a resistance to my possessive tendencies.

In Chapter Four, the ethical condition opened up by the face of the other is explored following Levinas' analysis in the earlier chapters. But here, I carry the analysis beyond Levinas to examine what happens after the moment in which the other appears. In Levinas, the other contests my desire. This means that the self is suddenly given a moral choice; I can either follow my inclination and attempt to possess the other, or I can respond to his presence and recognize him as an end-in-himself, as someone who is not there simply for my enjoyment. Thus, the encounter with the other makes me concretely free. Levinas stops his analysis at this moment, noting that when the law is inscribed within the self by the other, the self is set free, though endowed with an ought in the same gesture.

More is needed, however, to complete the story and carry Levinas' existential grounding of ethics to a system of morality and law. By focusing on what happens in my freedom—what my possibilities are in this freedom—and what occurs as a result of my positive response to the other, I return Levinas' existential grounding of ethics to Kant's rational and systematic approach. This transition, however, is not without its problems. Kant's ethics manifestly requires a suppression of the individual in favor of the universality of the law. Levinas' ethics unfolds in the immediate relationship between concrete individuals, self and other immediately facing each other, and therefore outside the universal domain of reason—that is, outside the domain of Kantian ethics. At first, it looks like Kant and Levinas are irreconcilable. But by appealing to Kierkegaard, I justify this transition from Levinas' description of moral experience to Kant's analysis of morality's essence.

Finally, I attempt to explain the intimate connection between self-esteem and generosity that was left unclarified in Chapter Two. Having established that a complete and integrated individual worthy of self-esteem becomes independent only in deference to the other, it becomes possible to ground a relationship between self and other that does not deny the exteriority of the other as the rational relation does. Having found a mode of being in which the human being is not alone, Levinas has overcome the extreme isolation of rational subjectivity indicated in Chapter One. We are not alone as individuals in the world, provided that our individuality is sealed in the only manner in which it can be, in deference to the other. Thus, the complete individual depends on the other for his independence. The opposition between dependence and independence is dissolved, and both self and other are preserved. Consequently, they are now able to relate to one another in concrete terms, and solipsism is overcome. Though I will depart from Levinas in this final chapter, I try to do so without obscuring his central message, namely that the interpersonal relation of the face-to-face is prior to the rational order, that ethics, and not ontology, is first philosophy. Thus, the other person is given as other prior to the rational order that later questions her existence.

*   *   *

I would like to thank Ned Beach, Dick Connolly, Julia Galbus, Kate Inskeep, Grant Jenkins, John Jones, Thomas Prendergast and Alan Sanders for assisting me with various aspects of this manuscript.

Chapter One

The Scandal of Philosophy

One of the central issues motivating Levinas' work concerns Western philosophy's attempt to understand human experience in terms of rationality. This approach imposes strict limits on any inquiry into human experience because it implicitly denies any meaningful relationship with something beyond self-consciousness. Admittedly, at the outset, Levinas' critique seems questionable. How does reason foreclose on relationships beyond consciousness? The answer to this pressing question lies in the tradition to which Levinas belongs. This tradition finds its early ancestry in Descartes and Kant, though it does not emerge as its own achieving its canonical form until Husserl and Heidegger. Since Levinas' contributions to philosophy follow from his critique of this tradition, it is necessary to begin here with it. Only then can we understand Levinas' important departure from it.

Readers who are well-acquainted with the phenomenological tradition will find this chapter to be a fairly standard interpretation of the thinkers in question. Since I begin Chapter Two with a concise summary of the current chapter, those who are already familiar with Descartes, Kant, Husserl and Heidegger may want to skip this chapter and begin with the next.

Descartes and the Discovery of Rational Subjectivity

Descartes begins the *Meditations*, "Some years ago I was struck by the large number of falsehoods that I had accepted as true in my childhood, and by the highly doubtful nature of the whole edifice that I had subsequently based on them."[1] In what follows, he informs his reader that the goal of the present inquiry is to purge himself of these falsehoods, find a starting point for rational inquiry that is true beyond doubt, and then rebuild his knowledge on this certain foundation. He begins by doubting all that can reasonably be doubted, hoping that the attempt to doubt the possible claims about reality will present him with something that cannot be doubted.

Doubting every possible claim about reality would certainly take a lifetime. But Descartes realizes that he can focus on the foundations of his knowledge, noting that "[o]nce the foundations of a building are undermined, anything built on them collapses of its own accord" (*PWD* II 12). The first foundational element that Descartes questions is whether things are as they appear. He considers the possibility that all of his perceptions of reality might be images in a dream. At the moment, he does not think he is dreaming. But then he remembers the countless times when what he thought was reality turned out later to be a dream. If it is possible that he is dreaming now, then it is reasonable to doubt that what he perceives now is not as it appears.

After doubting other elements of his knowledge that do not concern us here, Descartes realizes that in order for him to think, one thing must be true. He must exist. He writes, "*I am, I exist*, is necessarily true whenever it is put forward by me or conceived in my mind" (*PWD* II 17). The claim is so true that to doubt it is absurd. One cannot meaningfully claim, "I doubt that I exist," since in order to doubt, this being must exist. So, Descartes has found a claim that is beyond doubt. He then sets out to discover what else might be known with certainty.

He asks, "But what then am I?" and answers, "A thing that thinks. What is that? A thing that doubts, understands, affirms, denies, is willing, is unwilling, and also imagines and has sensory perceptions" (*PWD* II 19). But since Descartes is only a thinking thing, he has no body. Without a body, he cannot possibly have "sense perceptions," taking the term to mean a process by which the human being is informed about extra-mental affairs. After the dream argument, "perception" refers to impressions only insofar as they are in the mind. Descartes does not doubt that he is having perceptions, only that they refer to a world beyond him. He writes that this I

> is also the same 'I' who has sensory perceptions, or is aware of bodily things as it were through the senses. For example, I am now seeing light, hearing a noise, feeling heat. But I am asleep, so all this is false. Yet I

certainly *seem* to see, to hear, and to be warmed. This cannot be false; what is called 'having a sensory perception' is strictly just this, and in this restricted sense of the term it is simply thinking. (*PWD* II 19)

Sense perceptions, doubts, affirmations, inclinations of the will, and images within the mind have all now been redefined (by the very act of withdrawal and not arbitrarily by Descartes) as acts of thinking, as ideas. So, along with the discovery of the *ego cogito*, Descartes also discovers a related field of ideas that belongs to this thinking thing. Together, the *ego cogito* and its field make up what the tradition will call "rational subjectivity."

The field of ideas that belongs to the thinking self appears to be like the world of sensible experience. Even after withdrawing from the senses, Descartes still has a world, one that appears as real as the one existing prior to the condition of withdrawal. Thus, in the act of thinking, the "real" world is redefined as an "ideal" world, though Descartes never looses his conviction that there is another world beyond this ideal one and that the project of knowledge is to determine the precise relationship between these two worlds. Even so, much is at stake in treating the real as the ideal; most notably, where the world of sensibility "contained" other things and people that had an independent existence apart from the self, the world of rational subjectivity is self-centered, a world in which nothing "other" than the self can exist. If objects had an independent existence prior to their identification with an idea in the mind, afterwards, in knowledge, they have lost their status as other. Thus, Levinas, who is completely Cartesian in this regard, continually characterizes the process of coming to know something as the reduction of what is other to the self. "Knowledge is always an adequation [an equating] between thought and what it thinks. There is in knowledge, in the final account, an impossibility of escaping the self . . . " (*EI* 60).

The isolation of the self in thinking, along with the retention of a world, raises the question of whether or not objects in the ideal world are at all like real, extra-mental objects. This question is altered slightly when Descartes realizes that he could create the objects that appear to him, thereby forcing a more dramatic question about whether there are independently existing objects at all. From the perspective of the *ego cogito,* all reality must be confronted alone; there can be no other being. At least this is how the situation appears initially.

Descartes continues the *Meditations*, attempting to escape rational subjectivity by constructing a proof for the independent existence of God. Such a proof would mean that Descartes is not the only being there is. He begins by examining the ideas that belong to his mind; they may be regarded in two ways. The first is to take them formally or actually *as ideas*. "In so far as the ideas are considered simply as modes of thought, there is no recognizable inequality among them: they all appear to come from within me in the same fashion" (*PWD* II 27-28). The formal reality of the idea is the same for each idea since, for Descartes, "formal reality" means simply that a thing exists, and ideas exist.

The second way to consider ideas is to examine the object in the idea. "But in so far as different ideas are considered as images which represent different things, it is clear that they differ widely." The idea of an elephant differs from the idea of the sun respecting their content. Both are ideas and are, therefore, the same formally, but one is an idea of an elephant and the other an idea of the sun, and so they are different objectively.

Ultimately, objects in ideas fall into three metaphysical classes: there are ideas of modes or accidents (modifications), like ideas of sensual qualities such as blue, hot, smooth, etc. There are ideas of finite substances, such as ideas of dogs, chairs, pieces of wax and even the idea of Descartes himself. Finally, there is the idea of an infinite substance. The objective reality in the idea of a modification is less than the objective reality in the idea of a finite substance, which has less reality still than the objective reality in the idea of an infinite substance. Thus, the idea of blue, the idea of Descartes and the idea of God are ranked in this sentence increasingly in terms of their objective reality. "Descartes" in the idea of Descartes is more real than "blue" in the idea of blue. "God" in the idea of God is even more real.

At this point, Descartes appeals to a maxim of Medieval physics.

> Now it is manifest by the natural light [of reason] that there must be at least as much reality in the efficient and total cause as in the effect of that cause. For where, I ask, could the effect get its reality from, if not from

the cause? And how could the cause give it to the effect unless it possessed it? It follows from this both that something cannot arise from nothing, and also that what is more perfect—that is, contains in itself more reality—cannot arise from what is less perfect. (*PWD* II 28)

Descartes is suggesting that the effect of a cause can never have more reality than its cause. Thus, the cause of a finite substance must be a finite substance or an infinite substance. It cannot be a modification, because a modification contains less reality than a finite substance. Since this maxim is true for things taken formally, Descartes thinks it must also be true for objects in ideas. " . . . [I]n order for a given idea to contain such and such objective reality, it must surely derive it from some cause which contains at least as much formal reality as there is objective reality in the idea" (*PWD* II 28-29). This claim (which Descartes says is "transparently true") needs clarification.

The causal principles that apply to things also apply to objects in ideas, but when we consider these ideal objects, it must be true that they have actual (and not merely ideal) causes. Thus, the cause of "blue" in the idea of blue must be a cause taken actually. And since there must be as much reality in the cause as in the effect, the cause of the "blue" in the idea of blue must have formally as much reality as the idea has objectively. Thus, the actual cause of the "blue" in the idea of blue must have as much formal reality as a mode or accident. The same reasoning is used to determine possible causes for ideas of finite substances taken objectively. The cause of the "sun" in the idea of the sun must have the formal reality of a finite or infinite substance. A mode or accident does not have enough reality to cause this idea taken objectively.

The argument reaches its conclusion when Descartes asks about the possible cause of the idea of God, an infinite substance. This cause, which must have as much reality formally as the idea has objectively, cannot be a mode or accident, nor can it be a finite substance. This means, then, that Descartes could not have made up the idea of God himself. The only possible cause for the idea of God is an infinite substance. In turn, an infinite substance must exist formally in order to cause the idea of an infinite substance taken objectively. So, God must exist. The only way Descartes could possess the idea of God is for God to have put this idea in his mind. So he writes, "It is true that I have the idea of substance in me in virtue of the fact that I am a substance; but this would not account for my having the idea of an infinite substance, when I am finite, unless this idea proceeded from some substance which really was infinite" (*PWD* II 31).

Having established the existence of God, Descartes responds to a possible objection that a reader might make: an infinite being may be thought to exist simply on the basis of negating the idea of the finite. From the existence of the finite, then, one could derive the idea of the infinite, contrary to what the proof establishes. Descartes responds:

> . . . I clearly understand that there is more reality in an infinite substance than in a finite one, and hence that my perception of the infinite, that is God, is in some way prior to my perception of the finite, that is myself. For how could I understand that I doubted or desired—that is, lacked something—and that I was not wholly perfect, unless there were in me some idea of a more perfect being which enabled me to recognize my own defects by comparison? (*PWD* II 31)

The reason that the idea of the infinite cannot simply be the negation of the finite is that the situation must be precisely the reverse. The idea of the finite is the negation of the idea of the infinite. The latter is prior, and so the idea of a perfect being precedes the idea of an imperfect being. Otherwise the imperfect being could not know that it was imperfect.

The point is more easily understood when we realize that what Descartes means by "perfect" is "complete." A being that suffers from a desire is not complete. It lacks. But Descartes is aware of his own lack. This implies an unfulfilled *telos* that can only become an object of knowledge when the *telos* is known, yet not attained. This privation is reaffirmed continually by the idea of infinity. The contemplation of an infinite substance will continually reveal a lack in my being.

For most of our ideas—all but one—the idea itself does not reveal this lack. But the idea of an infinite substance is the idea of a being that cannot be comprehended or thought. Thus, there is always more in the idea than is thought. In Descartes' own terms, there is always more objective reality in this idea than formal reality. So, Descartes' awareness of his inability to comprehend God, that is, his awareness of the limits of his own reason—its finiteness—requires that the idea of God be prior to the idea of himself. Otherwise, he would think that he knew all things: " . . . if I derived my existence from myself,[2] then I should neither doubt nor want, nor lack anything at all; for I should have given myself all the perfections of which I have any idea, and thus I should myself be God" (*PWD* II 33).

To summarize, the existence of an idea that contains more objective reality than Descartes has formal reality indicates the presence of an idea that Descartes could not have created himself. This idea could only proceed from an infinite being who must actually exist. Therefore, God exists. Furthermore, since this idea is always incomplete—it is the thought of that which cannot be thought and, as such, it is an incomplete thought—the idea of an infinite substance indicates that I am a finite substance. This means, in turn, that the idea of God must be prior in me to the idea of myself.

Had Descartes wanted a more radical conclusion, he could have noted that the impossibility of thinking completely the idea of an infinite substance along with the desire to do so indicates that an *encounter* with this infinite substance must be prior to my act of thinking. This, in fact, will be the route that Levinas takes when he notes that the face-to-face encounter with the other person is prior to the entire order of knowledge. He writes:

> In the access to the face there is certainly also an access to the idea of God. In Descartes the idea of the Infinite remains a theoretical idea, a contemplation, a knowledge. For my part, I think that the relation to the Infinite is not a knowledge, but a Desire. . . . Desire is like a thought which thinks more than it thinks, or more than what it thinks. It is a paradoxical structure, without doubt, but one which is no more so than this presence of the Infinite in a finite act. (*EI* 92)

Levinas will later characterize this desire as metaphysical; it is the desire for the otherness of the other. As such, it can never be satisfied, for the possession of the other can never give me the *otherness* of the other. This very otherness is precisely what is lost in the act of possession. Thus, the desire for the other is always unsatisfied. The situation here is not unlike Descartes' idea of infinity which is forever an idea that cannot meet its *telos*.

In both Descartes and Levinas, the idea of the infinite transcends the isolation of the *ego cogito*, for it always entails that the self is not alone. Descartes' proof for the existence of God means that Descartes is not the only being there is. After this proof, he is no longer a solipsist. In what remains of the *Meditations*, he will argue that since God is perfect, he cannot be deceitful. Deceit is a sign of a lack, hence, an imperfection. So, God must have made him in such a way that, through the careful use of his rational faculty, he can reach the truth. On this basis, Descartes will argue in the last meditation that he probably has a body and that there probably is an external world that is much like the world he perceives in his mind. But his attention is not on these issues. He writes:

> The great benefit of these arguments is not, in my view, that they prove what they establish—namely that there really is a world, and that human beings have bodies and so on—since no sane person has ever seriously doubted these things. The point is that in considering these arguments we come to realize that they are not as solid or as transparent as the arguments which lead us to knowledge of our own minds and of God, so that the latter are the most certain and evident of all possible objects of knowledge for the human intellect. (*PWD* II 11)

The knowledge of the self and the knowledge of the existence of a being other than myself—whose existence is given apart from a knowledge of his essence—is prior and more certain than knowledge of the extra-mental world, including my own body. The self in relation to an absolute other precedes all things; knowledge of the extra-mental is founded on this relationship. Thus, in the *Meditations*, Descartes engages in *first* philosophy by tracing the origins of the known world back to a prior relationship between a finite and infinite being. This is the insight that Kant, Husserl and Heidegger fail to recognize. Yet, it is will be what Levinas recognizes so clearly.

Kant and the Phenomenal World Hypothesis

Following Descartes, Kant thinks that the discovery of rational subjectivity entails the acceptance of idealism as the starting point for philosophy.

Furthermore, beginning with idealism seems to require a proof for the existence of the external world. Kant writes in *The Critique of Pure Reason*:

> However harmless idealism may be considered in respect of the essential aims of metaphysics . . . it still remains a scandal to philosophy and to human reason in general that the existence of things outside of us . . . must be accepted merely on *faith*, and that if anyone thinks good to doubt their existence, we are unable to counter his doubts by any satisfactory proof.[3]

The quote is crucial for our purposes because it indicates that Kant does not accept Descartes' path out of the isolated mind, though he seems to accept his discovery of it. This is partly due to the nature of Kant's project, which sought to determine how experience of objects is possible. In attempting to isolate the conditions necessary for the experience of objects, he discovers certain concepts, called *categories*, that must be presupposed prior to experience. There are twelve such categories, divided into four groups of three. First there are the categories of quantity: unity, plurality, and totality. Second, there are the categories of quality: reality, negation, and limitation. Third are the categories of relation: those concerning inherence and subsistence, causality and dependence, and community (that is, reciprocity between agent and patient). Finally, there are the categories of modality: possibility and impossibility, existence and non-existence, and necessity and contingency. The ego uses these concepts to organize objects within experience, that is, to "constitute" objects and the relations between them. In this way, the ego makes objects ready to be known prior to any experience of them as objects.

Kant's realization that objects must be prepared for experience by the ego sets him on the verge of one of the most important discoveries in the history of philosophy, namely, that the "real" world is phenomenal. It contains objects as they appear in experience and not as they are in themselves. I may ask about the true nature of the lamp before me as it is apart from my experience. But it is impossible that I should have any knowledge of this sort, since all knowledge now applies only to objects as they are experienced, and so already conditioned by thought. I may like to make claims about how objects are causally connected apart from my experience of them. But insofar as cause and effect are applied to sense data prior to my experience of objects, it is impossible to determine what of cause and effect, if anything, belongs to the object outside of experience. The world that is known is only the world of objects as they appear in experience.

On the hypothesis that the real world is a phenomenal world—"reality" is a category, so it only applies to appearances—Kant ends speculative metaphysics. This ancient branch of philosophy sought to understand realities beyond human experience, such as the existence of God, the nature of the soul, etc. Since inferences to what must be the case apart from experience are impossible, Descartes' proof for the existence of God has a serious flaw. When he argues that God must have caused an idea within him, he is employing the category of cause and effect beyond the realm of appearances. Thus, Kant thinks that Descartes discovered the problem of the external world's existence, though he has not provided a proof that it exists.

This gesture that ends speculative metaphysics is expressed in the *Critique of Pure Reason*. But initially, in Kant's *Inaugural Dissertation*, the categories of thought were applicable to the extra-mental. If the categories applied to the extra-mental, then, at least on principle, it would be possible that once the categories were discovered, one could subtract them, as it were, from experience and what remained would belong to the thing-in-itself. These would be sense impressions that the ego accepted passively. Apparently, Kant was not satisfied with this analysis of how concepts related to the extra-mental. On 21 February 1772, he confessed to Hertz:

> In the *Dissertation* I was content to explain the nature of these intellectual representations in a merely negative manner, viz. as not being modifications of the soul produced by the object. But I silently passed over the further question, how such representations, which refer to an object and yet are not the result of an affection due to that object, can be possible.[4]

Presumably, the *Critique of Pure Reason* was composed to answer this question.

For Kant, part of the solution to this problem lies in correctly articulating the interplay between sensibility and understanding. "Objects are *given* to us by means of sensibility," he writes, "and it alone yields us *intuitions*; they are *thought* through the understanding, and from the understanding arise *concepts*" (*CPR* 65). Where before we could understand what the extra-mental provided by examining what remained after the categories of thought had been subtracted from experience, now the procedure must be much more complicated. Now it is necessary to re-trace the cognitive steps involved in concept formation back to sensibility. The idea is that by carefully examining the links between the processes involved in arriving at knowledge, we might recover something that the external world gives to knowledge. But, the links between sensible intuition and the understanding and between sensibility and sensible intuition are problematic. This issue sets the agenda for the discussion to follow. But before we can determine the relationship between the understanding and sensible intuition, it is necessary to define them.

Kant writes, "In whatever manner and by whatever means a mode of knowledge may relate to objects, *intuition* is that through which it is in immediate relation to them, and to which all thought as a means is directed" (*CPR* 65). Intuition, then, is that through which knowledge is "in immediate relation" to objects. But, Kant notes that there are two varieties of intuition, intellectual and sensible. Robert Paul Wolff summarizes this distinction:

> If the object depends upon the mind, then the mind is active with regard to it, and because of Kant's identification of the active or spontaneous with the intellectual, such relation is given the title 'intellectual intuition.' Alternatively, the mind may wait passively upon the object, and establish relation to it only in so far as it affects the mind. This capacity for being affected by objects is entitled 'sensibility,' and the product of such affection is 'sensible intuition.'[5]

Thus, sensible intuition is the means by which an object, derived from sensation, is situated in immediate relation to knowledge.

Initially, it may seem that Kant, by definition, has established a relationship between the extra-mental object and the mind through the use of sensible intuition. However, the capacity to be "affected by objects is entitled 'sensibility,' and the product of such affection is 'sensible intuition'." In turn, this means that the first appearance that the object makes to the mind is in sensible intuition *and not in sensibility*. Consequently, when we note that Kant has established a relationship between the mind and the object, "object" must be construed here as an appearance and not as an extra-mental object. The reasons why this is the case will be apparent in what follows.

Sensible intuition is resolvable into two components: "the material element, *which is purely subjective and cognitively valueless, is* sensation" (Wolff 73); the other is the formal element which gives knowledge and "is the spatio-temporal ordering of the sensations" (Wolff 73). Kant argues that we can strip away from a sensible intuition in general all that is present materially, and this will leave us with the pure forms of sensible intuition "in which all the manifold of intuition is intuited in certain relations [and] must be found in the mind *a priori*" (*CPR* 66). This division leaves us with two means of dealing with sensible intuition in general. Wolff suggests that "after dividing representations into intuitions and concepts, and intuitions into the sensible and the intellectual, we can finally distinguish pure sensible intuitions from empirical sensible intuitions, or perceptions" (Wolff 73). This division will be important because it indicates that sensible intuition in general is not an immediate relationship between the mind and the independently real, nor is it an immediate relationship between the mind and sensation. This is because sensible intuition is synthetic, that is, it is not functional until sensations are brought together and unified in a single manifold of consciousness by the *a priori* pure forms of sensible intuition, space and time, which condition sensations and prepare them for use by the understanding.[6] Inasmuch as sensible intuition is "synthesized" by the pure forms of sensible intuition prior to the experience of an object, the first appearance of the object to the understanding is already extended in space and time. Consequently, the object which is presented to the understanding is already conditioned, already unified in a manifold of sensible intuition, and it can now only be given as an appearance. Kant writes:

> Time and space, taken together, are the pure forms of all sensible intuition, and so are what make *a priori* synthetic propositions possible. But these *a priori* sources of knowledge, being merely conditions of our sensibility, just by this very fact determine their own limits, namely, that they apply to objects only in so far as objects are viewed as appearances, and do not present things as they are in themselves. (*CPR* 80)

This means that sensible intuition is unable to account for an immediate relationship between the mind and the independently real. So, it must be accounted for elsewhere, perhaps by the relationship between sensation and sensible intuition. Though Kant thought that such a relationship existed, sensation now falls beyond the domain of experience as is clear from Kant's notion that experience is always of objects, and objects are already conditioned by the pure forms of space and time. Since anything beyond space and time is no longer a legitimate topic of inquiry, questions concerning sensation are also illegitimate.

Even if sensible intuition arises from sensation immediately (a metaphysical claim), there is a problem in comprehending the relationship between sensible intuition and the understanding. Since the categories are *a priori* rules for the synthesis of appearances (which are themselves already conditioned by the pure forms of space and time), their employment beyond appearances is impossible. Thus, insofar as "existence" is in the "Table of Categories," it makes no sense to predicate existence to a realm beyond space and time. Thus, it becomes problematic, at best, to claim that sensations emerging from the independently real have an affect on the mind and as such are responsible for the material content of sensible intuitions.[7]

Nonetheless, it is clear from the early part of the *First Critique* that Kant did not wish to deny the existence of the independently real. In fact, "[t]he theory of the first half of the *Critique* cannot even be stated without presupposing the existence of the independently real" (Wolff 312). But, its existence is called into question in the later part of the *Critique* by the way in which Kant characterizes the concept of a "noumenon":

> What our understanding acquires through this concept of a noumenon, is a negative extension; that is to say, understanding is not limited through sensibility; on the contrary, it itself limits sensibility by applying the term noumena to things in themselves (things not regarded as appearances). But in so doing it at the same time sets limits to itself, recognizing that it cannot know these noumena through any of the categories, and that it must therefore think them only under the title of an unknown something. (*CPR* 273)

The *Critique* is marked with a central incompatibility regarding this notion of the noumenal. On the one hand, Kant wishes to assign a positive existence to the noumena whereby a noumenal self can interact with a noumenal world, thereby constituting the phenomenal world. On the other hand, the noumenal can function only as a concept with no positive existence of its own. This points out a serious contradiction in the *Critique*. As Körner indicates:

> If . . . we conceive, with Kant, a *noumenon* or thing in itself as being not only a non-phenomenon but something which somehow affects our senses, then our concept is no longer merely negative. Kant's assertion that in the *Critique of Pure Reason* he uses the concept of a *noumenon* only as a negative and limiting concept is thus incompatible with its actual use.[8]

The result is that Kant is an idealist, if we can take his claim that the "noumenal" is only a "limiting concept" seriously, and I think we must. There is no doubt that Kant was aware of this implication. In the "Antinomy of Pure Reason" he openly accepts the title of "transcendental idealism" which he distinguishes from "empirical idealism":

> [E]mpirical idealism finds no difficulty in regarding [appearances of inner sense in time] as real things. . . . Our transcendental idealism, on the contrary, admits the reality of the objects of outer intuition, as intuited in space, and of all changes in time, as represented by inner sense. (*CPR* 440)

At first, it looks like Kant's "transcendental idealism" overcomes the limits of subjectivity because it "admits the reality of objects of outer intuition." But, given the continual claims that "[s]pace itself, with all its appearances, is . . . only in me" (*CPR* 349) found in the "Paralogisms of Pure Reason" and the subsequent claim in the "Antinomies" that "[t]he objects of experience . . . are *never* given *in themselves*, but only in experience, and have no existence outside it" (*CPR* 440), it is difficult to find a relevant difference between this "transcendental idealism" and other varieties of idealism where the question of the existence of extra-mental objects is concerned.

If Kant is forced into idealism, which precludes positing the existence of the independently real, (regardless of Kant's intentions to posit the existence of such a realm), then the question of whether or not sensible intuition allows an immediate relationship between the mind and the independently real is moot. If, on the other hand, we grant to Kant the existence of the independently real as something that ultimately conditions sensible intuition, then sensible intuition, nevertheless, will be unable to satisfy our need to find a means to tie representations to extra-mental realities. The reason for this is that sensible intuition remains representational.

Inasmuch as the objects of sensible intuition are conditioned by the *a priori* forms of space and time and available to consciousness only as representations, the mind has no recourse to anything over and above a representation whereby it can claim that ideas, are, in fact, representations of objects in the extra-mental world. If we maintain that sensible intuitions represent sensations, then we must consider what sensations represent. They cannot represent objects in space and time, since sensation is prior to sensible intuition. If we claim that they represent the extra-mental world, then we have merely asserted that ideas are ultimately representations of the extra-mental world and that such a world exists. This world falls completely outside the domain of the knowable, and the scandal of philosophy—that it has been unable to furnish a proof for the existence of the external world—is still in place. Indeed, if Kant is correct to include the category of existence in the table of categories, then *the question itself cannot meaningfully be asked.* It, too, falls into the domain of speculative metaphysics.

In spite of the above mentioned difficulties, Kant's discovery that the real world is phenomenal should not be minimized. For one, it indicates that we do not need to undertake a method of doubt to place ourselves within the parameters of rational subjectivity. The equation of the real world with the known or knowable world—a precondition for all knowledge—has already placed us in this position. Secondly, it indicates that the category of existence does not extend beyond the known world. It is incorrect to speak of unexperienced things as either existing or not existing. So, if something other than the self and its phenomenal world "exists," it must "be" beyond the categories of being. This latter observation will make the encounter with the other a deeply religious and noumenous affair in the works of Levinas and partly explains the title of Levinas' last major work, *Otherwise than Being or Beyond Essence.*

Much of the confusion in Kant arises from his tendency to reduce all experience to rational experience. In Kant, there is no analysis of experience *as it is lived.* Non-cognitive elements of human lived-experience such as eating and drinking, bathing in pleasures and pains, crafting things out of raw materials, etc. simply do not have a place in Kant's view of world-formation. Because of this lack, his analysis has an intellectualist air to it and is, therefore, at odds with a holistic approach to experience. In the next section, we will see that this trait also belongs to Husserl. Indeed, it differentiates both Kant and Husserl from Levinas.

Kant does not consider the fact that not all human experience unfolds in the phenomenal realm. There are moments of experience in which the human being encounters unrepresented realities, uncategorized "things," that elicit emotional reactions apart from our knowledge of the world. These experiences indicate another order of existence, an order in which "things" "are" apart from the mind. Levinas, unlike Kant, will return to this level of experience to explain the relationship between the self and the extra-mental domain.

Husserl and the Phenomenological Reduction

In one sense, it is unfair to expect Husserl to account for how ideas relate to the extra-mental. His findings in the *Cartesian Meditations* and *Ideas* were not presented as answers to our question; rather he sought to describe and explain the sense of various experiences. Husserl brackets any questions of the independent existence of the external world. If he is not concerned with whether or not the extra-mental exists, then the relationship between ideas and the extra-mental cannot be a principal concern either. Nonetheless, Husserl discovers a way of approaching philosophy that is pertinent to our purposes.

Husserl's approach to analyzing consciousness, the phenomenological method, begins with "the epoché," the bracketing of existential questions. His intent is to use it strictly as a methodological device in a larger project of rendering "'pure' consciousness accessible to us . . . "[9]

> If I keep purely what comes into view—for me, the one who is meditat-ing—by virtue of my free epoché with respect to the being of the experi-enced world, the momentous fact is that I, with my life, remain untouched in my existential status, regardless of whether or not the world exists and regardless of what my eventual decision concerning its being or non-being might be.[10]

The effect of the epoché is that it reduces all experience to the phenomenal world and accomplishes what Husserl calls the "phenomenological reduc-tion." This reduction situates Husserl within an isolated consciousness, the same type of consciousness that Descartes uncovers in the *Meditations* after the dream argument.

Remaining true to the methodological play of the epoché, Husserl notes that the experienced world depends on consciousness. Where Descartes turns towards God to find a creator, even of the phenomenal world, Husserl turns to the ego. The ego creates its world in an act of world-constitution. In this act, the entire world is reduced to subjectivity. Husserl writes, "This *reduc-tion to my transcendental sphere of particular ownness* or to my transcen-dental concrete I-myself, by abstraction from everything that transcendental constitution gives me as Other, has an unusual sense. . . . *I 'alone'* remain" (*CM* 93).

Husserl does not think that his claim is too radical, for in no way does subjectivity alter the sense that the world is "experienceable by everyone" (*CM* 93). Though my "sense" is that the world is experienceable by every-one, the "world" here arises from transcendental constitution and, as such, is entirely *mine*. Likewise, my consciousness also constitutes the "sense" of the other person as one who is able to experience the world. Husserl finds him-self with a problem here that he attempts to solve by appealing to intersub-jectivity and the community of "subjects" who participate in it.

Intersubjectivity presupposes the other, but this presupposition is not of a really independent other. Instead, the other is present merely in an "objec-tive sense" and constituted as "co-present." Since this is only in sense, the other falls into a world that is dependent on *my* mind. Consciousness makes present "a 'there too', which nevertheless is not itself there and can never become an 'itself-there'" (*CM* 109). In the Husserlian system, the other person is not the extra-mental other. Thus, Schutz says of Husserl, "The transcendental 'constitution of the World' presupposes its existence in intersubjectivity which, by definition and method, does not exist for the transcendental ego in his supreme solitariness."[11]

While Husserl thinks that he avoids the problem of solipsism, he is, nevertheless, unconcerned about any idealistic consequences of his theories (at least before the writing of the *Crisis*), for his aim was not to locate the independent other or the extra-mental world, but to give an account of the "sense" that the world has for [his?] consciousness. Many people must have objected to his approach thinking that the sense of the world could not be understood without taking questions of existence into account. Speaking on behalf of the objectors, Husserl writes, "Without admitting that it does so, [phenomenology] lapses into a transcendental solipsism; and the whole step leading to other subjectivity and to genuine Objectivity is possible only by virtue of an unacknowledged metaphysics, a concealed adoption of Leibnizian traditions" (*CM* 148). He responds:

> [P]henomenal explication is nothing like 'metaphysical construction'; and it is neither overtly nor covertly a theorizing with adopted presuppositions of helpful thoughts drawn from the historical metaphysical tradition. It stands in sharpest contrast to all that, because it proceeds within the limits of pure 'intuition', or rather of pure sense-explication based on a fulfilling givenness of the sense itself. (*CM* 150-151)

In other words, Husserl here reasserts his starting position, namely that phenomenology begins with the phenomena and the constitution of this phenomena in a domain of meaning; it is not concerned with the metaphysical status of the phenomena themselves. So, properly speaking, Husserl is not a solipsist with respect to the existence of objects outside of consciousness. Even so, he remains a solipsist with respect to meaning. This latter point differentiates Levinas from Husserl. The existential status of objects apart from experience is irrelevant to Husserl's analysis of human experience. More so,

it is irrelevant to the very constitution of meaning itself. This claim is star-
tling because it means that other people, taken as subjects in themselves, are
also irrelevant to meaning in my life. They simply do not have a role. Husserl is forced to this position, according to Levinas, because consciousness
constitutes the world only in intentional relationships.

To say that consciousness is intentional is to say that all consciousness
must be consciousness of objects. It is also to say that objects are only objects for consciousness; they are constituted as objects in the very act of
knowing. So, it is impossible that there can "be" an extra-mental object, to
speak precisely. *Prior to knowledge there is no object* that can assist me in
the constitution of meaning. Meaning is entirely the result of my doing.

Levinas praises Husserl for realizing these points: in Levinas' language
they mean only that Husserl is turning away from a naturalist conception of
being to a phenomenological one. Here, being and its categories are ascrib-
able only to objects in the known world, much as Kant's categories were. But
Levinas also notes that Husserl's story is incomplete. It is mistaken to the
extent that it takes all relationships to operate in a theoretical and intentional
manner. In his desire to make philosophy an exact science, Husserl reduces
consciousness to knowing and consequently removes it from the cares of
daily life as it is lived. (Husserl himself was aware of this consequence, and
so he turns to the *Lebenswelt*, the life-world, in his later works.)

All is not lost, however, for Husserl provides a thorough analysis of
representational consciousness, a proper topology of rational subjectivity. He
accurately describes what happens in the act of knowing. For Levinas, the
reduction to my "sphere of ownness" is radical; the phenomenological reduction occurs implicitly every time the human being turns away from living to
reflect on living. It is not simply a methodological device, but an expression
of existential transformations that occur in the human being upon entry into
the realm of thought. Thus, knowing essentially isolates the mind from the
extra-mental domain; it is a withdrawal of the mind from the senses, to
express the same principle in Descartes' terms. Levinas' critique of Husserl
follows from this realization. Husserl begins philosophy with the phenomenological reduction; thus, he begins too late in the process of knowing and does

not consider what prompts the person to turn away from sensual life and towards the isolation of thought. The pre-conditions of the phenomenological reduction are left undisclosed. So, Levinas concludes his *The Theory of Intuition in Husserl's Phenomenology:*

> [D]espite the revolutionary character of the phenomenological reduction, the revolution which it accomplishes is, in Husserl's philosophy, possible only to the extent that the natural attitude is theoretical. The historical role of the reduction and the meaning of its appearance at a certain moment of existence are, for him, not even a problem.[12]

Levinas' philosophy is directed precisely at the pre-conditions for the reduction. Prior to the intentional relation, that is, prior to thought, unfolds another kind of meaning that Husserl neglects. As we will see in the next section, Heidegger deepens Husserl's understanding of meaning by turning to the structures of human existence rather than limiting himself to the structures of thought. But he will not go far enough.

Heidegger and the Critique of Representational Consciousness

Heidegger, like Levinas, criticizes Husserl for reducing human experience to the experience of objects. Husserl is forced to do this because of his strict adherence to the doctrine of intentionality. The doctrine states, again, that all consciousness must be consciousness of objects. Furthermore, since these objects are now understood as the creation of the ego's theoretical act, Husserl has reduced the world to the transcendental ego. There is nothing outside of it. This tendency to reduce the world to "objects" of the constituting and intentional power of consciousness has another, more pressing, consequence; it takes the world to be a collection of objects while treating the world itself as an object. These objects are made to be objects by consciousness in the act of thinking them; they are not "there" beforehand as objects, though they may be constituted as having-been-there-beforehand.

Heidegger responds to Husserl by translating Husserl's phenomenology into the language of ontology and raising again the fundamental question of metaphysics: what is the meaning of Being in general? He notes that Hus-

serl's "objects" of consciousness are, first of all, entities or beings one encounters within the world. Until we understand the meaning of Being in
general, it is impossible to understand how a particular entity is or what it
means for it to be. It cannot simply be taken as an object whose existential
status is irrelevant. One must know how it came to be and the manner in
which it is before it can be understood at all. (How can I know what it
means for a being to be, without knowing what Being in general means?)
Thus, where Husserl forgets the question of Being entirely, Heidegger demonstrates the necessity of raising it again.

In *Being and Time*, Heidegger sets out to forge this "fundamental ontology." After demonstrating the importance of raising again the question of
Being on the grounds that no one as of yet has answered it and few have
even asked it, he notes that Being, though always the being of an entity, is
never itself an entity. It never emerges as an object, though it conditions all
objects. Since it cannot be reduced to a content of an intention or the object
of a representation, it does not fit neatly into Husserl's categories of existence. Furthermore, and more importantly, Being cannot be thought along
conventional lines since to do so, as Husserl has so nicely pointed out,
means that it must be taken as an object. Thus, the path to understanding the
meaning of Being in general cannot be discursive; a much more circuitous
route is needed.

How then might the human being find access to Being, if it cannot be
thought in the way that entities can be thought? Heidegger's answer to this
question is that we approach Being hermeneutically by asking that "entity
which in its Being has this very Being as an issue"[13] for it. This entity is
privileged over and above that kind of entity that has no concern for its
being. The former is human being—Heidegger's *Dasein*—the latter are
things. Where the ontological tradition has based its inquiry on beings who
are not concerned about their being, that is, on mere things, Heidegger reverses direction arguing that the way in which Dasein *is* affects the way that
beings are for it. If entities are given as objects in Husserl's system, this is
only because one of the modes of Dasein's Being is to represent things as
objects. Only after an adequate understanding of the Being of Dasein can we

truly understand the Being of entities and, more specifically, how they come to be. So, Heidegger sets out on an analysis of Dasein. This project takes up the first half of *Being and Time*.

Heidegger begins Chapter One:

> We are ourselves the entities to be analyzed. The Being of any such entity is *in each case mine*. These entities, in their Being, comport themselves towards their Being. As entities with such Being, they are delivered over to their own Being. *Being* is that which is an issue for every such entity. This way of characterizing Dasein has a double consequence. (*BT* 67)

The second of these consequences, that "[t]hat Being which is an *issue* for this entity in its very Being, is in each case mine" does not concern us here, but the first does, that "[t]he 'essence' of this entity lies in its 'to be'" (*BT* 67). Heidegger adds, "Its Being-what-it-is (*essentia*) must, so far as we can speak of it at all, be conceived in terms of its Being (*existentia*)" (*BT* 67). He goes on to note that the term *existentia* cannot be taken in its traditional usage. Traditionally, it means "presence-at-hand," a type of Being that belongs to things or objects. To differentiate Dasein's Being from the Being of things, Heidegger reserves the term "*existentia*" for Dasein while letting "Being-present-at-hand" name the Being of things.

If Dasein is to be understood as it is essentially, then it is necessary to examine its existence structures, that is, its modes of Being. Heidegger calls these structures "*existentialia*," which though analogous to Kantian categories, are different from them. The categories belong to an inquiry into beings-present-at-hand. They belong to beings designated by a "what," the beings that populate Husserl's world of intentional objects. Dasein, however, has a different character of Being. It is not merely present to itself, and it is never present to itself in the way that a mere thing is. The *existentialia* comprise a list of ways of Being for Dasein. Some of these are Being-in, Being-alongside, Concern, Solicitude, Mood, Understanding, Possibility, and Discourse. Each provides a clue to the Being of Dasein. The project of the "Dasein Analytic" is to make these structures explicit so that Dasein's Being can be clarified, ultimately with the aim of understanding Being in general.

Two levels of existence are now apparent in Heidegger's work. The first is the level of objects present-at-hand, the things in the world, understood by means of the categories through intentional acts of representation. The second is the level of Dasein understood from within its experience, not as an object of its own consciousness, but as a Being that exists in certain ways and knows that it exists in these ways, not through representation, but by immediate acquaintance, that is, by being what it is. These two levels of existence come to bear dramatically on what it means for Dasein to be in the world in which it encounters things.

On the way to determining what it means for Dasein to be in-the-world, Heidegger distinguishes between taking Being-in-the-world categorically and taking it existentially. Being-in-the-world taken categorically is spatial and designates the relationship of one present-at-hand thing included in another present-at-hand thing in the way that a piece of furniture is in a house. Heidegger notes that such a mode of Being cannot belong to Dasein: "[t]here is no such thing as the 'side-by-sidedness' of an entity called 'Dasein' with another entity called 'world'" (*BT* 81). Though such a characterization articulates the Being of things, even this cannot properly be understood until a deeper ontological understanding is made explicit.

Heidegger notes that opposed to a categorical understanding of Being-in, an existential understanding treats Being-in as dwelling or residing. Here, the relationship is not spatial. It refers instead to the way in which Dasein lives in the world and attends to matters of its existence. Some of the ways in which Dasein dwells in the world are "having to do with something," "producing something," "attending to something and looking after it," "making use of something," "interrogating," "considering," "discussing," "determining," etc. Though these are various modes of Being-in-the-world, they are all modes of concern. This means, in turn, that Dasein as an entity concerned about its Being must be analyzed prior to any attempt to articulate its Being as "rational animal." First we are concerned about our existence; the quest for knowledge and its fulfillment in representation is but one way in which we exhibit this concern. Having articulated Being-in-the-world existentially as concern, Heidegger turns to examine knowing insofar as it is founded upon concern.

In knowing, objects present themselves as present-at-hand; they are articulated by means of categories. These categories supply certain relational structures to existence, most notably the relationship between subject and object. To view Dasein as a Being-in-the-world in the way that the contained is in the container is to take Dasein as a representation, and not to consider it existentially. Only within knowledge is the category of "inside" and "outside" present. Thus, the belief that all reality is reducible to understanding—a belief that seems to be present in Kant and Husserl—and the subsequent tendency to take thoughts on the "inside" to be articulations of the world on the "outside" reduces the human being to the transcendental ego and objects to thoughts within this ego. Only in the grip of such a reduction "can the problem arise of how this knowing subject comes out of its inner 'sphere' into one which is 'other and external' . . . " (*BT* 87). Indeed, this is precisely the problem that motivated Descartes to question his beliefs in the *Meditations*, that brought Kant to pronounce an end to speculative metaphysics, and that led Husserl to believe that philosophy could unfold within the horizons of the phenomenological reduction. The problem and its solution is stated by Heidegger: "Knowing is a mode of Dasein founded upon Being-in-the-world. Thus Being-in-the-world, as a basic state, must be Interpreted *beforehand*" (*BT* 90). Simply put, this means that an existential analysis of Dasein must be prior to a characterization of it as knower, and, once again, metaphysics is prior to epistemology.

The tendency to reverse the priority of these two classic philosophical discourses in Kant is what has presented the necessity of proving the existence of the external world. Kant reduces human experience to subjectivity and then is perplexed about how consciousness goes from "inside" subjectivity to some region "outside" of it. Indeed, it is precisely this concern that motivates Kant's attempt to redefine the world phenomenally so that he can explain the possibility of knowing the world. Thus, responding to Kant's observation that "it still remains a scandal to philosophy and to human reason in general that the existence of things outside of us . . . must be accepted

merely on *faith* . . . " (*CPR* 34) and his subsequent attempt to provide a
"proof" for such things, Heidegger writes:

> . . . if one were to see the whole distinction between the 'inside' and the
> 'outside' and the whole connection between them which Kant's proof pre-
> supposes, and if one were to have an ontological conception of what has
> been presupposed in this presupposition, then the possibility of holding that
> a proof of the 'Dasein of Things outside of me' is a necessary one which
> has yet to be given, would collapse.
>
> The 'scandal of philosophy' is not that this proof has yet to be given,
> but that *such proofs are expected and attempted again and again.* (*BT* 249)

Heidegger's analysis of Dasein's Being as concern and his characterization
of knowing as a mode of Being founded on concern establishes a relationship between Dasein and its world prior to the insertion of the categories of
subject and object in knowledge. Prior to knowing, Dasein dwells in its
world; the world is no object among objects, and Dasein is not a subject that
thinks representations. What then is Dasein and its world and how do they
relate prior to knowledge? In Husserl's terms this is to ask about the human
being in relation to its surroundings prior to the phenomenological reduction.

Heidegger answers this question by characterizing Dasein primarily as a
doer and only secondarily as a knower. (In other works, Heidegger uses the
term *homo faber*, from the Latin *faber* meaning a worker or craftsman, to
describe the human being in place of the traditional *homo sapiens*.) Dasein
is fundamentally concerned with entities that it encounters in its environment
to the extent that they are useful for some purpose or another. Entities taken
in this sense "are not thereby objects for knowing the 'world' theoretically;
they are simply what gets used, what gets produced, and so forth" (*BT* 95).
Heidegger calls them "equipment" and notes that no piece of equipment
exists in isolation from all the others. "Equipment—in accordance with its
equipmentality—always is *in terms of* its belonging to other equipment" (*BT*
97). The computer that I am using to write this manuscript gathers its meaning as equipment by relating to (and hence refers implicitly to) the keys that
I am pressing, the printer, the pen I will use to mark proof copies, the hand
that will hold this pen, the publisher, the reader, etc. Though "[t]hese 'Things'
never show themselves proximally as they are for themselves . . . " (*BT* 97-

98), they are nonetheless implicated in a totality of references that point back to the computer as a tool.

Heidegger calls the Being of these tools "readiness-to-hand" and contrasts it to any "outward appearance" that an entity may possess in vision or in knowledge. No matter how much we might stare at a coffee cup or understand what it is theoretically, its readiness-to-hand will never manifest itself. This can only be found in the using or the availability for using that the entity possesses. Even so, our dealing with these tools is not blind. "[I]t has its own kind of sight, by which our manipulation is guided and from which it acquires its specific Thingly character" (*BT* 98). This sight is called "circumspection" (*Umsicht*). Circumspection is quite another type of seeing than that which is typically attached to visual seeing or the construction of a world of objects in knowledge. These latter modes understand objects only insofar as they are present-at-hand. The significant difference between the two modes is that in circumspection the embeddedness of a tool in a referential context with other tools is always a part of a tool's function. Understanding an object theoretically, or viewing it as a thing in vision, severs the interconnections between things and isolates them as individuals.

Because these tools in their functions all refer back to the work that is to be produced, they also point back to the worker, Dasein, and any other Dasein who are at all connected with my work.

> Thus along with the work, we encounter not only entities ready-to-hand but also entities with Dasein's kind of Being—entities for which, in their concern, the product becomes ready-to-hand; and together with these we encounter the world in which wearers and users live, which is at the same time ours. Any work with which one concerns oneself is ready-to-hand not only in the domestic world of the workshop but also in the *public world*. (*BT* 100)

Thus, as a worker, or to speak more appropriately, in its working, Dasein is thoroughly embedded in a vast interconnection of references that makes it impossible to separate Dasein from everyone and everything else. Here, on this level of existence, there is no worker as subject against which his production, or those for whom it is produced, or the things by which it is produced, can be called objects. These categories of subject and object will not emerge in the world until there is a break in the process of working, as when Dasein is done for the day and turns to contemplate its accomplishments, or when a piece of equipment turns up missing or no longer functions as it should.

In a section of *Being and Time* appropriately titled, "How the Worldy Character of the Environment Announces itself in Entities Within-the-world," Heidegger discusses this break away from function. He notes that there are three modes of this break from the equipmental totality that "have the function of bringing to the fore the characteristic of presence-at-hand in what is ready-to-hand" (*BT* 104). They are conspicuousness (*Auffälligkeit*), obtrusiveness (*Aufdringlichkeit*), and obstinacy (*Aufsässigkeit*). What is ready-to-hand becomes conspicuous when a particular tool is broken or cannot perform the function that I am trying to assign to it. It becomes obtrusive when I reach for a tool and "it *turns up* missing," to use a colloquial expression. The tool in these cases is present in its absence, and it exhibits a greater presence directly proportional to the urgency with which I want it. In both of these cases what is ready-to-hand turns out to be unready-to-hand. Sometimes, something that is unready-to-hand presents itself as an obstacle to another project, as when I encounter something that must be done before I do another project. "Anything which is unready-to-hand in this way is disturbing to us, and enables us to see the *obstinacy* of that with which we must concern ourselves in the first instance before we do anything else" (*BT* 103).

In each of these instances, the implicit reference of the tool to other tools and to the task at hand is disturbed. The function of the tool announces itself. We become aware of what the hammer is for when it no longer functions as a hammer. " . . . *[W]hen an assignment has been disturbed*—when something is unusable for some purpose—then the assignment becomes explicit" (*BT* 105). Along with it, the purpose of the work and the entire system of references is "lit up." The hammer presents itself, along with the work and the client who will be delayed, etc. Heidegger writes, "The context of equipment is lit up, not as something never seen before, but as a totality constantly sighted beforehand in circumspection. With this totality, however, the world announces itself" (*BT* 105). In other words, the world in which Dasein dwells is revealed precisely in a break away from it, but the break itself still preserves a connection with what was there beforehand. What emerges as present-at-hand in the world as an object for a theme still retains its implicit reference back to other objects, tools, Dasein, etc. Because of this referring back, the world of present-at-hand entities is not without foundation. No proof is needed for its existence, for the meaning of its Being relies upon and is given in this referring back. Thus, Heidegger writes:

> . . . if the world can, in a way, be lit up, it must assuredly be disclosed. And it has already been disclosed beforehand whenever what is ready-to-hand within-the-world is accessible for circumspective concern. The world is therefore something 'wherein' Dasein as an entity already *was*, and if in any manner it explicitly comes away from anything, it can never do more than come back to the world.
>
> Being-in-the-world, according to our Interpretation hitherto, amounts to a non-thematic circumspective absorption in references or assignments constitutive for the readiness-to-hand of a totality of equipment. (*BT* 106-107)

If Dasein is already "in" the world, then the question of the existence of the world seems somehow inappropriate, even if knowing the world reduces the world to representation and removes Dasein from the work-a-day world that defines it existentially.

What is critical here, and this point must be underlined, is that *Heidegger, in fact, accepts the characterization of reason presented by Descartes, Kant and Husserl.* Reason *is* representation, and in reason the world of Dasein and its equipment becomes reified into a world of subjects and objects. His point of disagreement is that his predecessors do not understand that knowing is *founded* upon Being-in-the-world, and that this means that the world is given in knowledge even if it cannot be conceived and taken up as a theme. So where the world of the ready-to-hand is the world in which Dasein dwells in a totality of interconnected relatedness with everything else, the world understood in reason severs this interrelatedness and creates subjects and objects. In reason, then, the categories of "inside" and "outside" are born.

In Husserl's terms, the phenomenological reduction distorts the world in which the human being lives. Husserl's phenomenology does not simply describe human experience; it forces this description to take certain directions. Heidegger notices the error and tries to deepen the phenomenological method by taking a broader perspective on experience. In doing so, he notices that the phenomenological reduction occurs naturally when the human being takes up knowledge and reifies its thinking into objects. Thus, this reduction cannot be merely a methodological device; it occurs in a broader context of life. We see then that Levinas' concern that Husserl does not inquire into the "historical role of the reduction and the meaning of its appearance at a certain moment of existence" is shared somewhat by Heidegger, though in a provisional manner. For Heidegger, the reduction occurs as a break away from the world of function that is prompted by a disturbance in the totality of assignments on the level of equipment. For Levinas, it is a reaction to the unrepresented intrusion of some unknown X into my world. It is a response to the foreign other that must always come from beyond Heidegger's equipmental totality.

This most important difference between Heidegger and Levinas stems from a fundamental disagreement over the basic structure of human experience. Where Heidegger observes that the human being dwells in-the-world in concern, Levinas characterizes a being that is kept awake by the vigilance of insomnia, to speak in metaphorical terms. Moreover, where Heidegger places Dasein into an intricate web of equipmental assignments and references, Levinas returns to the level of the body, to sensibility, to characterize the human being as an entity that lives within the elemental qualities of the environment. It bathes in music, is enchanted with the play of lights, feels the wind blow over the surface of its skin, and all of this in a fundamental act of possession, of supreme enjoyment, of egoistic play. Thus, Levinas writes:

> Enjoyment—an ultimate relation with the substantial plenitude of being, with its materiality—embraces all relations with things. The structure of the *Zeug* [tool] as *Zeug* and the system of references in which it has its place do indeed manifest themselves, in concerned handling, as irreducible to vision, but do not encompass the substantiality of objects, which is

always there in addition. Moreover furnishings, the home, food, clothing are not *Zeuge* in the proper sense of the term: clothing serves to protect the body or to adorn it, the home to shelter it, food to restore it, but we enjoy them or suffer from them; they are ends. Tools themselves, which are-in-view-of . . ., become objects of enjoyment. The enjoyment of a thing, be it a tool, does not consist simply in bringing this thing to the usage for which it is fabricated—the pen to the writing, the hammer to the nail to be driven—but also in suffering or rejoicing over this operation. . . . To enjoy without utility, in pure loss, gratuitously, without referring to anything else, in pure expenditure—this is the human.[14]

To be sure, Heidegger has forgotten the body and the sensuality of living from the environment. He has forgotten his childhood, for in childhood, the desire to know is not a mode of concern, but of play. More importantly, however, he has forgotten that prior to the work-a-day world of using tools and building things, functions had to be inscribed within me. I had to learn the function of a hammer from a teacher without whom I would not be able to work.

In the next chapter, I will return to Descartes' philosophy of sensibility, for Descartes sees the departure into reason as a withdrawal from the body and the irrational life of sensibility. Unlike Heidegger, who characterizes life outside of reason as a dwelling among tools, this life, for Descartes, belongs to the body and to sensation.

Chapter Two

The Horizons of Cartesianism

The previous chapter was dedicated to the relationship between the mind and the extra-mental domain as laid out by Descartes, Kant, Husserl and Heidegger. There, it was noted that in pure intellection the mind has no recourse to the extra-mental. The reduction of all experience to reason, or representation, is what allowed the question of the external world's existence to emerge in the first place. The "scandal of philosophy" was, according to Heidegger, that in limiting experience to reason, philosophy forced this question. Prior to representing realities, the human being dwells in the world. Knowing is, thus, founded on this Being-in-the-world. Once this is remembered, it seems quite extraneous to inquire about the existence of the external world; it is given as part of the structure of human experience.

But, if the question of the external world's existence arises when we reduce experience to rational experience, then we have learned something important about the structures involved in knowing the world. Knowing succeeds only by breaking away from Being-in-the-world. That is, knowledge is isolation; "it is still and always a solitude" (*EI* 60). Though knowledge might begin as a mode of Being-in-the-world, it succeeds by turning its back on these origins and entering upon another terrain. Thus, Heidegger's recourse to the external world could not be within knowledge. Instead, he grounded it in concern, the primordial way in which the human being dwells in the world. Knowing is but one way in which the human being exhibits this concern, and a very limiting way at that. Where Husserl showed the limits of representation to be within the parameters of the transcendental ego, Heidegger pushed the frontiers of the world down to another level, the level of function.

On this level, the human being dwells as a worker; things are construed as implements for-the-sake-of something else. These implements refer to other implements in a referential totality guided by "circumspection." The world of function is held together as a totality by an intricate web of references, each pointing to others. The hammer refers to the nail, to the thing being produced, to the person for whom it is made, etc. Of course, none of this is apparent until after something disturbs the totality, causing functions to appear within the phenomenologically-reduced world of the present-at-hand.

In pursuing human being to the level of function, Heidegger thinks that he has found the most primordial levels of being human (or, at least, the most primordial levels necessary to answer the question of the meaning of Being). But it would seem that Heidegger has forgotten that before I can pick up a hammer and use it in a matrix of function, I must first learn the function of a hammer. Prior to the world of tools comes another order of existence. Prior to being a craftsman, I am an apprentice, a student who learns at the hands of another. Prior still, I am a being who takes delight in my tools, who builds things with them as a child at play, not for the sake of something else, but because it is entertaining in itself. When I grow up (and put childish things aside) the matrix of tools will change; but I do not begin here in this world of function; I enter into it from somewhere else. There are, in other words, levels more primordial than the level of function.

One of these levels belongs to the body and sensibility. This domain of existence—which appears in the works of the twentieth century French Cartesians, such as Merleau-Ponty and Sartre, and is absent in the works of their German counterparts, Husserl and Heidegger—lies outside the rational order. According to Descartes, on the level of practical life, mind and body form a unity held together by sentient existence. Where Heidegger characterizes knowing as a break away from Being-in-the-world, Descartes characterizes it as a "withdrawal from the senses," that is, a withdrawal from practical and sentient life. At the same time, this withdrawal separates the mind from the body. In order to understand this transformation from practical to theoretical life, it is necessary to examine more closely Descartes' thoughts on mind-body unity and the process of withdrawal. This examination constitutes the topic of the current chapter.

In a letter to Princess Elizabeth of Bohemia, Descartes confesses that he has "said hardly anything" about mind-body unity (*PWD* III 218). Indeed, his comments on the matter are scattered throughout his corpus. Often fragmentary and quite obscure, they speak a common theme, namely that mind and body form a "substantial union" and that sensation is possible only for a mind-body composite. In a letter to Regius, Descartes writes that "the union which joins a human body and soul to each other is not accidental to a human being, but essential, since a human being without it is not a human being" (*PWD* III 209). In the same letter he writes that "sensations such as pain are not pure thoughts of a mind distinct from a body, but confused perceptions of a mind really united to a body" (*PWD* III 206). He goes on to note that an angel in a human body "would not have sensations as we do." In a letter to Gibieuf, he notes that animals, like angels, do not have sensations, though the explanation he provides for their absence in animals is different from the one for angels (*PWD* III 203-204). The significance of these observations is that mind-body unity is a deeply human affair. Beings so united are neither angels nor animals, but, more importantly, neither are they spiritual substances placed within material ones. The union of mind and body is a third kind of thing, namely, a human being, who is a substantial composite of two types of substances intimately interrelated in a common project of sensation. In turn, the mind separated from the senses, that is, the *ego cogito*, cannot be a human being. It "does not have sense-perception strictly so called" (*PWD* III 380). Even though Descartes indicates a "real distinction" between body and mind, and that a mind in isolation does not have sensations, he maintains their substantial union.[1] Clearly, two different ways of regarding existence are present in Descartes' work. There is the embodied, sentient life of the human being and the disembodied, rational life of the *ego cogito*.

Descartes notes that the disembodied life of the *ego cogito* results from an act of "withdrawing the mind from the senses." Indeed, this act is "a prerequisite for perceiving the certainty that belongs to metaphysical things" (*PWD* II 115). Descartes is so convinced of this fact that he notes that the arguments waged for the existence of God in the *Discourse* are "obscure only to those who cannot withdraw their mind from their senses . . . " (*PWD* III 53). Furthermore, Descartes advises Silhon to "detach his thought from things that are perceived by the senses," if he wishes to understand the metaphysical truths of the *Discourse* (*PWD* III 55). Later, in a letter to Vatier, Descartes blames the obscurity of the *Discourse* in part on the fact that he did not "say everything which is necessary to withdraw the mind from the senses" (*PWD* III 86).

The method of doubt as presented in the *Meditations* is an improvement on the process of withdrawal as presented in the *Discourse*. In the "Synopsis of the following six Meditations," Descartes writes, "Although the usefulness of such extensive doubt is not apparent at first sight, its greatest benefit lies in freeing us from all our preconceived opinions, and *providing the easiest route by which the mind may be led away from the senses*" (*PWD* II 9. Emphasis mine). This concern about withdrawing the mind from the senses is so central to Descartes that he will mention it in two other prefatory texts to the *Meditations*, once in the "Dedicatory letter to the Sorbonne" and again in the "Preface to the reader."[2] He mentions the same concern to Mersenne (see *PWD* III 164) and in several other places. In fact, this concern is raised so many times that it alone might explain the innovations of the *Meditations* over and above those of the *Discourse*.[3]

Descartes' characterization of disembodied experience is cast against the backdrop of his ideas concerning embodied experience. Though he never explains embodied experience as thoroughly as disembodied experience, he does provide us with a hint about its nature: it is intimately connected with the processes of imagination and sensation. In fact, it would seem that these processes tie the mind to the body, thereby making unified experience possible. Thus, before continuing with a characterization of embodied experience, it is first necessary to discuss how imagination and sensation tie the mind to the body. This requires us to distinguish thought, imagination and sensation from each other. In turn, these distinctions will explain why Descartes thinks that "withdrawing the mind from the senses" is a prerequisite for metaphysical inquiry and why such inquiry must be parasitic on mind-body unity.

Thought, Imagination and Sensation

Descartes defines "thought" to "include everything that is within us in such a way that we are immediately aware of it" (*PWD* II 113). Elsewhere, he enumerates various modes of thought.

> All the modes of thinking that we experience within ourselves can be brought under two general headings: perception, or the operation of the intellect, and volition, or the operation of the will. Sensory perception, imagination and pure understanding are simply various modes of perception: desire, aversion, assertion, denial and doubt are various modes of willing. (*PWD* I 204)

While pure understanding belongs to a mind separated from the senses, thoughts arising from imagination and sensation belong to a mind-body composite. Both of these rely on physiological factors, in the case of imagination, on a corporeal image in the brain, and in the case of sensation, on neurological movements within the human body.

Descartes defines imagining as "simply contemplating the shape or image of a corporeal thing . . . " (*PWD* II 19). There are two components of this act. On the one hand, there is the act of contemplation, and, on the other, there is the object contemplated. Contemplation is the act by which I am aware of a corporeal impression in the brain, and so, this act is a thought, but the object contemplated is not a thought. Descartes writes to Mersenne, "The forms or corporeal impressions which must be in the brain for us to imagine anything are not thoughts; but when the mind imagines or turns towards those impressions, its operation is a thought" (*PWD* III 180). Elsewhere, Descartes affirms that "in understanding the mind employs only itself, while in imagination it contemplates a corporeal form" (*PWD* II 264). He notes further that the difference between the powers of understanding and imagination is not merely a difference of degree. Rather the two are "quite different kinds of mental operation" (*PWD* II 264). The act of imagination requires both the awareness of a corporeal impression in the brain *and* the corporeal impression. In this manner, then, imagination is an act of a mind-body composite, with awareness belonging to the mind and the corporeal impression to the body.

In a letter to Mersenne, Descartes notes that "whatever we conceive without an image is an idea of the pure mind, and whatever we conceive with an image is an idea of the imagination" (*PWD* III 186). Sometimes the same object can be treated under both categories, though not in the same respect. A triangle, for instance, is an idea of the imagination insofar as I picture in my mind a three-sided figure with internal angles equaling 180 degrees. But I may also treat that triangle on a purely conceptual level and deal only with its mathematical properties, in which case it becomes an idea of the pure mind. Descartes uses the difference between a triangle and a chiliagon to make this point in the Sixth Meditation: a triangle is both understandable and imaginable, but a chiliagon, on the other hand, is understandable, though not imaginable, since in the imagination it is indistinguishable from a myriagon. So, Descartes says to Gassendi that "although geometrical figures are wholly corporeal, this does not entail that the ideas by means of which we understand them should be thought of as corporeal . . . " (*PWD* II 264). Indeed, they may be studied either by pure understanding or imagination. Under the auspices of pure understanding, we deal with geometrical figures only insofar as they are intelligible.

Though objects of imagination are intelligible as well—insofar as we are aware that we are imagining them, they must have a corresponding thought—there are some objects of the intellect that are unimaginable. Descartes explains to Mersenne, "As our imagination is tightly and narrowly limited, while our mind has hardly any limits, there are very few things, even corporeal things, which we can imagine, even though we are capable of conceiving them" (*PWD* III 186). Among these, Descartes places the idea of the soul and the idea of God. He explains to Mersenne that the soul is unimaginable, taking this to mean that it "cannot be represented by a corporeal image," though he goes on to note that this "does not make it any less conceivable" (*PWD* III 186).

The fundamental difference, then, between pure understanding and imagination lies in the fact that the former unfolds without a corporeal impression and, therefore, in a mind separated from its body. Imagination, on the other hand, requires both a corporeal impression and a thought. Thus, so long as I am imagining, I cannot retreat into any metaphysical domain of pure understanding, and my understanding of incorporeal things will always be confused.

The same relationship that makes imagination a mind-body affair also pertains to sensation, for it too will be made up of a combination of something arising from the body and an awareness of that something. Sensations include feelings of pleasure and pain, the passions of the soul, as well as the perceptions of color, sound, taste, touch, and smell. Again, insofar as I am aware of them, I am engaging in an activity of thought; but, insofar as they are necessarily present if I am to be aware of them at all, the body is deeply implicated in the process of sensation. Sensation, then, like imagination, is possible only for a mind-body unity.

Descartes' remarks on sensation are ambiguous, owing to the fact that sometimes by "sensation" he means a rational apprehension of the object of sense, what some philosophers refer to as perception as opposed to sensation, and, at other times, the passive process of receiving sense data. He clarifies this ambiguity in the "Sixth Set of Replies" by distinguishing three "grades of sensory response." The three grades shed light on the difference between sensation and thought. The first grade of sense "is limited to the immediate stimulation of the bodily organs by external objects" (*PWD* II 294). It is highly mechanical, and it is shared by both humans and animals. Descartes describes this sensory process with the example of seeing a stick. Here, "rays of light are reflected off the stick and set up certain movements in the optic nerve and, via the optic nerve, in the brain . . . " (*PWD* II 295). Since sensory response of the first grade is common to humans and animals and since animals do not think, that is, they are unaware of sense data, it must be the case that sensory response of the first grade does not involve thought. It, therefore, belongs strictly to the body and does not arise from the mind-body composite.

The second grade of sensory response differs from the first in that awareness is a part of the response. Descartes writes:

> The second grade comprises all the immediate effects produced in the mind as a result of its being united with a bodily organ which is affected in this way. Such effects include the perceptions of pain, pleasure, thirst, hunger, colours, sound, taste, smell, heat, cold and the like, which arise from the union and as it were the intermingling of mind and body, as explained in the Sixth Meditation. (*PWD* II 294-295)

This is "sensation" in the strict sense. It is constituted out of sensory qualities which are not, properly speaking, objects, but qualities that we attribute to objects. Since second grade sensory response unfolds in the mind as a result of bodily motions, such response requires that the mind and body be unified. Again, the mechanics of the body provide the content, while the mind provides the awareness of this content.

When we get to the third grade, thought begins to play a more dominant role. Descartes writes that "[t]he third grade includes all the judgements about things outside us which we have been accustomed to make from our earliest years—judgements which are occasioned by the movements of these bodily organs" (*PWD* II 295). He goes on to provide an example:

> . . . suppose that, as a result of being affected by [a] sensation of colour, I judge that a stick, located outside me, is coloured; and suppose that on the basis of the extension of the colour and its boundaries together with its position in relation to the parts of the brain, I make a rational calculation about the size, shape and distance of the stick: although such reasoning is commonly assigned to the senses (which is why I have here referred it to the third grade of sensory response), it is clear that it depends solely on the intellect. (*PWD* II 295)

The third grade, then, does not refer to sensation proper, but to judgments that are made on the basis of sensation. Furthermore, these are acts of the intellect alone.

The three grades of sense are distinguished on the basis of their "location" in either the body, the mind-body composite, or the mind. The first grade belongs to the body alone. The second is possible only when mind and body are unified, since this grade is precisely the awareness of a physical sensation. The third grade, though based on sensations of the second grade, is an act of the intellect, though habit has us forget this fact. Descartes writes:

> I demonstrated in the *Optics* how size, distance and shape can be perceived by reasoning alone, which works out any one feature from the other features. The only difference is that when we now make a judgement for the first time because of some new observation, then we attribute it to the intellect; but when from our earliest years we have made judgements, or even rational inferences, about the things which affect our senses, then, even though these judgements were made in exactly the same way as those we make now, we refer them to the senses. The reason for this is that we make the calculation and judgement at great speed because of habit, or rather we remember the judgements we have long made about similar objects; and so we do not distinguish these operations from simple sense-perception. (*PWD* II 295)

The distinction between the second and third grade is between sensations and judgments of sensations, between seeing color and attributing it to an object that exists beyond the mind and the body, out there, in an external world. A close reading of the *Meditations* and surrounding commentary by Descartes suggests that the preconceived opinions that are being called into doubt in this work are precisely these judgments based on sense-perception and which are not, properly speaking, sense-perception. In the *Meditations*, Descartes attempts to retract these judgments in order to see how much of our knowledge of the external world arises from sensation and how much from thought alone.

Indeed, Descartes points out that "bodies are not strictly speaking perceived by the senses at all, but only by the intellect" (*PWD* II 95). Elsewhere, he writes, "[The senses] normally tell us of the benefit or harm that external bodies may do to this [mind-body] combination, and do not, except occasionally and accidentally, show us what external bodies are like in themselves" (*PWD* I 224). Sensations of the second grade are experienced not as thoughts, but as an awareness of the grumbling in my stomach, for instance, that I identify as (or judge to be) hunger. Sensations of this kind are felt as pleasure or pain, warning me when to take action and when to pause. They do not provide truth; rather, they unfold outside the domain of essences as practical experiences that make up daily life. Descartes goes on to note that "[i]f we bear this in mind we will easily lay aside the preconceived opinions acquired from the senses, and in this connection make use of the intellect alone, carefully attending to the ideas implanted in it by nature" (*PWD* I

224). We have distinguished imagination and sensation from thought by showing that, for Descartes, both imagination and sensation are an awareness of something bodily. Insofar as the body provides that something and the mind the awareness, both sensation and imagination require mind-body unity. They are psycho-physical processes.

The term "thought" is used to include anything in me of which I am aware. Types of thought include my awareness of corporeal impressions produced by the brain, that is, imagination, and my awareness of mechanical motions within my body, that is, sensation.[4] But there is another type of thought which unfolds within me and whose object is nothing that requires a body. This is pure thought. Since metaphysical realities, like God and the soul, cannot be apprehended in sensation or imagination—they have no extension—they must be known by another mode of thought. Descartes writes to Gassendi that "the pure understanding both of corporeal and incorporeal things occurs without any corporeal semblance" (*PWD* II 265). But since some people have been biased by experience to equate "thing" with something extended, that is, imaginable, these people will never understand metaphysical realities. Once again, Descartes blames preconceived opinion. The reason people confuse "thing" with something imaginable is "because of the false preconceived opinion which makes them believe that nothing can exist or be intelligible without being also imaginable, and because it is indeed true that nothing falls within the scope of the imagination without being in some way extended" (*PWD* III 362). This observation is at the root of one of the central difficulties that Descartes will have to combat concerning his metaphysics. As early as the *Rules for the Direction of the Mind*, written in 1628, he notes that

> when the intellect is concerned with matters in which there is nothing corporeal or similar to the corporeal, it cannot receive any help from these faculties; on the contrary, if it is not to be hampered by them, the senses must be kept back and the imagination must, as far as possible, be divested of every distinct impression. (*PWD* I 43)

Metaphysical realities, even in the *Rules,* can only be understood by bracketing out corporeal impressions. Because many people limit existence to imaginable or sensible things, they will be unable to arrive at an understanding of such things as God and the Soul. Much later, in the *Principles*, published in 1644, Descartes writes:

> . . . many people's understanding of substance is still limited to that which is imaginable and corporeal, or even to that which is capable of being perceived by the senses. Such people do not know that the objects of the imagination are restricted to those which have extension, motion and shape, whereas there are many other things that are objects of the understanding. (*PWD* I 220)

Again, in the *Conversation with Burman:* "[t]he fact that there are some people who are clever at mathematics but less successful in subjects like physics is not due to any defect in their powers of reasoning, but is the result of their having done mathematics not by reasoning but by imagining—everything they have accomplished has been by means of imagination" (*PWD* II 352). Once again, we encounter a class of people that cannot retreat into a world of pure understanding and who will, therefore, never reach an adequate understanding of the *Meditations*. This is so in spite of the fact that the *Meditations* goes to great lengths to distinguish acts of imagination from those of pure understanding. This is the point of the "piece of wax" example at the end of the Second Meditation.

We can now better understand Descartes' concern about making sure that the readers of the *Discourse* and the *Meditations* practice "withdrawing the mind from the senses," if they are going to understand the proper subject matter of these two texts. The danger of not doing so is the irresistible temptation to think of metaphysical realities as imaginable ones and, therefore, misanalyze them. People who cannot understand things without the help of the imagination and sensation cannot understand realities such as God and the soul, because they are trying to understand something that does not accord with the kind of thought they are using. In fact, Descartes goes directly after the Aristotelian Scholastics on this point, because they believe there is "nothing in the intellect which is not first in the senses." His main target is Gassendi, who is trying to use the imagination to understand things that belong to pure thought alone. On the other end of the spectrum, it should be clear that pure thought is not the mode of thinking to be used when trying to understand mind-body unity. Since pure thought requires the separation of the mind from the body, using pure thought to understanding mind-body unity will undoubtedly present problems. Princess Elizabeth of Bohemia commits this error. Thus, we have here in Princess Elizabeth and Gassendi two types of error that shed light on the operations of thought, imagination and sensation as they pertain to the difference between embodied and disembodied existence. Gassendi uses imagination to understand things belonging to pure thought, and Princess Elizabeth uses pure thought to understand things belonging to sensation and imagination. Since Descartes' responses to each of these persons clarifies several important features of unity and disunity, it is appropriate to examine each case in some detail.

The Horizons of Metaphysical Inquiry and
the Life of the Body

On May 6th, 1643, Princess Elizabeth of Bohemia sent a letter to Descartes. After studying the *Meditations*, she could not understand how an immaterial mind could interact with a material body. So, she asked, "How can the soul of man, being only a thinking substance, determine his bodily spirits to perform voluntary actions?"[5] How can an immaterial mind exert its influence on a material body? Something immaterial can neither touch nor contact something material, and since Descartes explains bodily movements in terms of mechanical (and hence, physical) causes, the Princess should be perplexed. After some traditional niceties, Descartes responds:

> There are two facts about the human soul on which depend all the knowledge we can have of its nature. The first is that it thinks, the second is that, being united to the body, it can act and be acted upon along with it. About the second I have said hardly anything; I have tried only to make the first well understood. (*PWD* III 217-218)[6]

He summarizes the second in what follows. His answer to Elizabeth's question unfolds in two letters, the letters of May 21st, 1643 and June 28th of the same year.[7]

In both letters, Descartes begins by appealing to what he calls "primitive notions." In the first letter, he describes them as "the patterns on the basis of which we form all our other conceptions" (*PWD* III 218). There are some general ones "which apply to everything we can conceive" (*PWD* III 218). He names being, number and duration as examples. The remaining notions apply only to particular types of things we can conceive. " . . . [A]s regards body in particular, we have only the notion of extension, which entails the notions of shape and motion" (*PWD* III 218). What Descartes seems to be saying here is that when we conceive of bodies, we employ the notion of extension. Under this broader notion of extension are two sub-notions, shape and motion.

Descartes continues, " . . . [A]s regards soul on its own, we have only the notion of thought, which includes the perceptions of the intellect and the inclinations of the will" (*PWD* III 218). When we conceive of the soul, we employ the notion of thought. Thus, it is clear that different notions are used when we are thinking about the soul than are used when we consider bodies.

When we conceive of the union of body and soul, however, we employ neither the notions of thought nor extension. Descartes writes, "Lastly, as regards the soul and the body together, we have only the notion of their union, on which depends our notion of the soul's power to move the body, and the body's power to act on the soul and cause its sensations and passions" (*PWD* III 218). Thus, when we conceive of the person as a mind-body unity, we employ a different notion, that of their union.

In the second letter, these notions are enumerated differently. In addition, different "operations of the soul" are named "by which we acquire them" (*PWD* III 226). Here, Descartes names the notions of body, soul and the union between body and soul as the primitive notions. He aligns the intellect with the notion of the soul, the imagination with the body, and the senses with the union between soul and body. Thus, through the intellect we take possession of the notion of thought, and through the imagination we take possession of the notion of body. But only through the senses can we take possession of the union of soul and body. Thus, Descartes writes:

The soul is conceived only by the pure intellect; body (i.e. extension, shapes and motions) can likewise be known by the intellect alone, but much better by the intellect aided by the imagination; and finally what belongs to the union of the soul and the body is known only obscurely by the intellect alone or even by the intellect aided by the imagination, but it is known very clearly by the senses. (*PWD* III 227)

So, three distinct groups of notions are present, the notions of the intellect, the imagination and the senses.

Since the various operations of the soul employ different primitive notions, it should be clear that both the notions and their respective operations will be assigned to different modes of inquiry. In the first letter, Descartes expresses the necessity of employing the proper notion (and hence, the proper operation of the soul) for a particular inquiry. He writes, "I observe . . . that all human knowledge consists solely in clearly distinguishing these notions and attaching each of them only to the things to which it pertains. For if we try to solve a problem by means of a notion that does not pertain to it, we cannot help going wrong" (*PWD* III 218). If we wish to undertake an inquiry into the nature of bodies, we should employ the imagination and the respective primitive notions that belong to bodies, namely, extension, motion, and shape. If we should try to employ the notions assigned to the pure intellect, we are committing a methodological error. It would not be unfitting to call this type of error a category mistake. Other mistakes of this variety occur when "we try to use our imagination to conceive the nature of the soul, or we try to conceive the way in which the soul moves the body by conceiving the way in which one body is moved by another" (*PWD* III 218). When Elizabeth asks how the soul can act on and be acted upon by the body, she is guilty of the latter error.

Remaining true to the architecture established here, Descartes goes on to assign various inquiries to various notions.

Metaphysical thoughts, which exercise the pure intellect, help to familiarize us with the notion of the soul; and the study of mathematics, which exercises mainly the imagination in the consideration of shapes and motions, accustoms us to form very distinct notions of bodies. But it is the ordinary course of life and conversation, and abstention from meditation and from

the study of the things which exercise the imagination, that teaches us how
to conceive the union of the soul and the body. (*PWD* III 227)

Thus, the *Meditations* falls naturally within the horizons of the pure intellect, since the goal of that work is to reach an understanding of God and the soul. But the science of physics would be misplaced in this domain; it must make use of the imagination and the notions of motion, extension and shape. Understanding the union of body and soul, however, does not belong to any mode of inquiry—in actuality we do not *think* with our senses—but to the domain of practical life, to the domain in which we do rather than think.

Along these lines, Descartes seems to suggest that some people will be prone to use their pure intellect as their primary mode of "understanding" things—Elizabeth is one of these—while "people who never philosophize" employ their senses in understanding the world. These people "have no doubt that the soul moves the body and that the body acts on the soul" (*PWD* III 227). The incomprehensibility of mind-body unity indicates that Elizabeth is meditating too much, and so Descartes gives her the following word of advice:

> I believe that it is very necessary to have properly understood, once in a lifetime, the principles of metaphysics, since they are what gives us the knowledge of God and of our soul. But I think also that it would be very harmful to occupy one's intellect frequently in meditating upon them, since this would impede it from devoting itself to the functions of the imagination and the senses. I think the best thing is to content oneself with keeping in one's memory and one's belief the conclusions which one has once drawn from them, and then employ the rest of one's study time to thoughts in which the intellect co-operates with the imagination and the senses. (*PWD* III 228)

Elizabeth's problem is that she is looking to find in pure thought something that cannot be found there. It cannot be found there because the entry into thought *means* the end of mind-body unity. And so Descartes responds:

> I think it was [the] meditations rather than thoughts requiring less attention that have made Your Highness find obscurity in the notion we have of the union of the mind and the body. It does not seem to me that the human mind is capable of forming a very distinct conception of both the distinc-

tion between the soul and the body and their union; for to do this it is necessary to conceive them as a single thing and at the same time to conceive them as two things; and this is absurd. (*PWD* III 227)

Yet, and this is the critical point, both can be conceived at different times. Two contradictory "truths" seem to arise from two different states of human being. Descartes has no trouble with the contradiction, since the analysis of reason undertaken in the *Meditations* and elsewhere indicates that reason must contradict the senses, at least respecting the question of the relationship between mind and body.

Since "all human knowledge consists solely in clearly distinguishing these notions and attaching each of them only to the things to which it pertains," it would seem that Elizabeth's error is that she is trying to apply the categories of the intellect—which are restricted to metaphysical inquiry—to the level of sensual life. Descartes suggests that mind-body unity can never be understood intellectually, since pure understanding itself uses a set of categories that have the net result of disembodying the mind. If Elizabeth wishes to "understand" mind-body unity, she needs to quit thinking so much and return to daily life.

In responding to Elizabeth, Descartes reaffirms his position on the essential difference between pure thought, imagination and sensation. But he goes beyond what was said earlier by noting that not only are these operations intrinsically different from each other; more importantly, certain types of inquiry belong to particular modes of thought. Once again, the necessity of "withdrawing the mind from the senses" is asserted, not merely because the senses are an obstacle to pure thought, but because there is an incompatibility between the type of thought used and the object at hand. The act of withdrawal facilitates metaphysical understanding by placing the thinker in the proper field of inquiry. Without careful attention to situating ourselves in the proper field of inquiry, we might be tempted to ask how something material can touch something immaterial, a question that can only emerge from trying to occupy contrary epistemic perspectives at the same time.

Gassendi makes a related error because he tries to understand the *Meditations* using analogies based on objects that are apprehended in the imaginative mode of thought. Because of this fact, Descartes seems not to take his objections seriously. He writes, "I think your purpose has . . . been to bring to my attention the devices which might be used to get round my arguments by those whose minds are so immersed in the senses that they shrink from all metaphysical thoughts" (*PWD* II 241). Later, Descartes accuses Gassendi of not having called into question his preconceived opinions and of misunderstanding the methodological necessity of withdrawing the mind from the senses. "When I said that the entire testimony of the senses should be regarded as uncertain and even as false, I was quite serious; indeed this point is so necessary for an understanding of my *Meditations* that if anyone is unwilling or unable to accept it, he will be incapable of producing any objection that deserves a reply" (*PWD* II 243). Clearly, Gassendi is one of these people.

Because Descartes considers Gassendi's objections misplaced, I will not take the time here to present them. However, in replying to them, Descartes clarifies many issues pertinent to our present purposes. To begin with, he states when doubting the senses is important and when it is not:

> . . . when it is a question of organizing our life, it would, of course, be foolish not to trust the senses, and the sceptics who neglected human affairs to the point where friends had to stop them falling off precipices deserved to be laughed at. Hence I pointed out in one passage that no sane person ever seriously doubts such things. But when our inquiry concerns what can be known with complete certainty by the human intellect, it is quite unreasonable to refuse to reject these things in all seriousness as doubtful and even as false; the purpose here is to come to recognize that certain other things which cannot be rejected in this way are thereby more certain and in reality better known to us. (*PWD* II 243)

The purpose of doubting the senses is to remove confusion and determine what can be known by pure thought. Naturally, the things that are best known are going to be those things that are most intimately associated with pure thought itself. This is why the mind is more clearly known than the body. This also explains what Descartes is doing in the *Meditations*, namely reducing all experience to the pure intellect by stripping out the bodily elements that make imagination and sensation possible *for the sake of under-*

standing unimaginable and non-sensible entities. He affirms this reduction in a comment to Gassendi concerning the *cogito*:

> . . . when I discover that I am a thinking substance, and form a clear and distinct concept of this thinking substance that contains none of the things that belong to the concept of corporeal substance, this is quite sufficient to enable me to assert that I, in so far as I know myself, am nothing other than a thinking thing. This is all that I asserted in the Second Meditation . . . (*PWD* II 245)

In so far as he knows himself, Descartes is a thinking thing. In fact, he did try in the *Meditations* to use his imagination to uncover his nature only to conclude that "none of the things that the imagination enables [him] to grasp is at all relevant to this knowledge of [himself] . . . " (*PWD* II 19).

Gassendi notes this passage in his objections and then goes on to say, "But you do not say how you recognize this. And since you had decided a little earlier that you did not yet know whether these things belonged to you, how, may I ask, do you now arrive at the conclusion just quoted?" (*PWD* II 185). Descartes replies, "'belonging to me' is clearly quite different from 'belonging to the knowledge which I have of myself'" (*PWD* II 247). Here, we have Descartes admitting that there may be more to his existence than what can be known. In turn, this means that, for the "rationalist" Descartes, not everything can be dragged into the domain of pure thought. Descartes is not the *ego cogito.* Rather, the ego *cogito* is the self reduced to knowledge.[8] This is a point that Gassendi seems incapable of grasping. He is trying to understand the immaterial soul, or mind, by an analogy with the body. But since the body is extended and not a thinking thing, it does not produce a quality analogous to a thinking thing. " . . . [T]he whole nature of the mind consists in the fact that it thinks, while the whole nature of the body consists in its being an extended thing; and there is absolutely nothing in common between thought and extension" (*PWD* II 248). Descartes ends his replies to Gassendi by accusing him of making one of the category mistakes discussed in reference to Princess Elizabeth earlier:

> At no point do you produce objections to my arguments; you merely put forward doubts that you think follow from my conclusions, though in fact

they merely arise from your desire to call in the imagination to examine
matters which are not within its proper province. (*PWD* II 266)

Gassendi is unable or unwilling to make the reduction to knowledge that
understanding the *Meditations* requires.

The import of all this is that in Cartesian philosophy we find (at least)
three horizons that govern human existence. Each horizon is determined in
reference to a particular variety of thought: pure thought has no recourse to
sensibility or imagination and, as such, it unfolds in the life of a disembodied
soul. But each of the others unfolds in reference to the body, and sensibility
to the mind-body composite, to the *whole* man. Properly speaking, then,
mind-body unity does not unfold within theory, since the entry into pure
thought *requires* the separation of mind and body, but only within practical
life. " . . . [I]t is the ordinary course of life and conversation, and abstention
from meditation and from the study of the things which exercise the imagination, that teaches us how to conceive the union of the soul and the body."
Merleau-Ponty aptly characterizes this lived body-soul unity. Speaking on
Descartes' behalf, he writes:

> The truth is that it is absurd to submit to pure understanding the mixture
> of understanding and body. These would-be thoughts are the hallmarks of
> "ordinary usage," mere verbalizations of this union, and can be allowed
> only if they are not taken to be thoughts. They are indices of an order of
> existence—of man and world as existing—about which we do not have to
> think.[9]

In addition to relegating sensible qualities to the mind-body composite,
Descartes also places the entire range of human passion on the same level.
Concrete human existence is understood, not through theoretical ideas, but
through acquaintance with passions. Descartes' final work, *The Passions of
the Soul*, analyzes existence on this level.

Passion and the Soul

Earlier, I noted that Descartes defined thought to "include everything that
is within us in such a way that we are immediately aware of it." He divided

these thoughts into two general categories, perceptions and volitions. Perception was further divided into sensory perception, imagination and pure understanding. In his last work, *The Passions of the Soul*, he upholds a similar topology, though he analyzes thought from a slightly different perspective. Here, thoughts are divided into actions and passions. Actions "are all our volitions, for we experience them as proceeding directly from our soul and as seeming to depend on it alone." The passions, in turn, are defined as "the various modes of perceptions or modes of knowledge present in us" (*PWD* I 335). These are passions because "it is often not our soul which makes them such as they are, and the soul always receives them from the things that are represented by them" (*PWD* I 335). They are opposed to actions because they arise involuntarily and because the soul is a "passive" recipient of them. Their source lies elsewhere.

Descartes indicates two sources of these perceptions: they are the effects of either the body or the soul. Perceptions caused by the soul are either perceptions of volition or perceptions of "all the imaginings or other thoughts which depend on them" (*PWD* I 335). He notes that since "it is certain that we cannot will anything without thereby perceiving that we are willing it," perceptions of volition are "really one and the same thing as the volition" (*PWD* I 336), though he acknowledges that these perceptions have both an active and passive component. As volitions, they are active. But, as perceptions, they are passive.

The "imaginings or other thoughts which depend on" volition occur "[w]hen our soul applies itself to imagine something non-existent . . . and also when it applies itself to consider something that is purely intelligible and not imaginable . . . " (*PWD* I 336). When the soul imagines something *at will* or turns its attention to metaphysical beings, like God and the soul, it is causing a perception, that is, a passion. But since "these things depend chiefly on the volition which makes it aware of them . . . we usually regard these perceptions as actions rather than passions" (*PWD* I 336). As in the perceptions of volition, the soul is affecting itself; it is both the agent and patient of its own action. So much for perceptions caused by the soul.

Perceptions caused by the body are divided into three categories: those of the external world, the body, and the soul. Perceptions of the external world are biological reactions to sense data which strike the sense organs, thereby causing movement in the nerves. Perceptions of the body are feelings of pleasure and pain which appear to be internal. Finally, perceptions of the soul are feelings which appear to be in the soul (e.g., anger, joy, etc.), and "for which we do not normally know any proximate cause to which we can refer them" (*PWD* I 337).

While all the types of perceptions caused by the body are "passions of the soul" taken in a broad sense, Descartes restricts the term "passions" to the third type, and defines them as "those perceptions, sensations or emotions of the soul which we refer particularly to [the soul], and which are caused, maintained and strengthened by some movement of the [animal] spirits" (*PWD* I 338-339). Passions in the strict sense, then, are reactions to physiological stimuli arising from the body and emerging in the soul as feelings such as anger, joy, generosity, esteem, etc. Though they are *caused* by the body, the are *referred* to the soul. Since a thought is anything of which we are immediately aware, and since the passions of the soul are thoughts caused by the body, the passions of the soul must collectively signify a mode of bodily awareness. But unlike the thoughts that represent objects for theoretical consideration, these thoughts "move and dispose the soul to want the things for which they prepare the body. Thus the feeling of fear moves the soul to want to flee, that of courage to want to fight, and similarly with the others" (*PWD* I 343). They are, in other words, motivational, experienced as force or compulsion rather than representation.

The passions present a mode of thought in which the soul attends to bodily considerations in a practical manner. The soul "understands" its passions, not in the mode of knowing an object, but in the mode of knowing whether that object will bring beneficence or harm. It understands the worthiness, value, or usefulness of an object for the human being. If the passions relate to objects in the mode of value, then they understand non-representationally. They do not represent "objects" in the phenomenologically-reduced world of pure thought. This is explicitly clear respecting the passion of wonder. Descartes opposes wonder, "the first of all the passions" (*PWD* I 350) to the apprehension of an object as known, and, therefore, familiar. Wonder arises "[w]hen our first encounter with some object surprises us and we find it novel, or very different from what we formerly knew or from what we supposed it ought to be . . . " (*PWD* I 350). Jean-Luc Marion aptly notes that if what inspires wonder is the novelty and unexpectedness of an object, then it is not the object itself that inspires the passion, but "the modality of its presence." So, in wonder, "[t]he object disappears behind the modality of its presence; in other words, the object of wonder is already no longer an object but a (necessarily unreal) modality of objectivity."[10] In wonder the human person comports himself towards the object of wonder non-theoretically, and similarly with the other passions.

Since the passions situate persons non-theoretically in relation to "objects," they do not reduce the world to pure thoughts. In passion the world is not reduced to the phenomenal world, to cast this observation in the language of Chapter One. Therefore, they open up a mode of "understanding" the world without forcing the separation between self and world that representation suggests. In turn, this allows the human being a mode of comporting itself towards objects concretely. In this mode, there is no room for questions concerning the real existence of the objects with which I am currently engaged, nor is there room for questions about the ontological status of my body. This follows naturally from the realization that the passions of the soul belong to perceptions of the second grade discussed above. Since the passions are physical processes of which I am aware—and, therefore, are psycho-physical processes—they unfold only in the life of an embodied being. In passion, the soul is incarnated in the body. Though I have not found Descartes to say so explicitly, I suspect that the same reason that makes imagination and sensation psycho-physical processes applies here as well, namely, that since passion is a type of awareness of a physical state, it is impossible to have a passion without both the awareness of the physical state and the physical state. Furthermore, if the very act of passion requires a body, then the body's existence is given in passion.

We can characterize passion as a non-representational awareness of the modality of an object's presence. It is also a mode of comportment for embodied beings in the concrete world. That I can hate an object that, at one time, I loved, indicates that love and hate do not represent the object as object, though they both respond to it in some way. The passions of the soul present the affective "color" of an object in relation to the self quite apart from the essence of that same object. The passions open up a mode of comportment towards things without the necessity of knowing what they are (as in wonder, for instance.) Were it not for this fact, it would be quite impossible to comport oneself towards an infinite and incomprehensible God.

Furthermore, since the passions of the soul belong to the third primitive notion discussed above—and hence, to the senses—and pure thought to the first primitive notion, and since the move to pure thought requires withdrawing the mind from the senses as a way of turning back against the "preconceived opinions of childhood," it must be the case that the human being begins embodied by passion and sensation. Only later do we take up theorizing as a departure from this concrete and practical point of view. The human being starts out embedded concretely *in the world*, prior to theorizing about it, even if the turn to theory, to pure understanding, can only unfold in an act of separating the mind from the body and departing from the world.

Descartes is profoundly aware of the differences between the concrete, practical thought of an embodied being using its intellect in cooperation with the imagination and the senses, and the theoretical mode of thought belonging to the *ego cogito* in consideration of metaphysical beings. Furthermore, he knows that the separation of pure thought from the body is a "process" of departing from the world of concrete concerns, and, hence, an act of withdrawing the mind from the senses.[11] This realization once again explains Descartes' concern about the inability of those who cannot withdraw their minds from their senses—and, thus, from their bodies—and so understand the reality belonging to metaphysical things, and "why people who never philosophize and use only their senses have no doubt that the soul moves the body and that the body acts on the soul" (*PWD* III 227). More importantly, it indicates that undertaking metaphysical speculation is a matter of retreating from practical life. Doing so impedes the soul "from devoting itself to the functions of the imagination and the senses" (*PWD* III 228). Where Husserl does not see "[t]he historical role of the [phenomenological] reduction and the meaning of its appearance at a certain moment of existence" as a problem (*TIHP* 157), Descartes is aware that the entry into pure thought—the entry into the phenomenologically-reduced world—alters the sense that the world has for experience. Indeed, this is precisely the point that he is trying to make to Princess Elizabeth and Gassendi. In short, this means that, for Descartes, entertaining the epoché must signal a change of perspective, a redirecting of thought into a theoretical realm that necessitates a departure from the life of the senses and from all that this entails. Neither Husserl's transcendental ego nor Descartes' *ego cogito* can have passions as can the embodied being.

Heidegger expands the horizons of the world to include the intricate connection of functions and shows that knowing is a departure from being in this realm. "Knowing is a mode of Dasein founded upon Being-in-the-world" (*BT* 90). This means that the phenomenological reduction that occurs naturally in knowledge arises from another perspective, that of the world of function. Descartes accepts a similar doctrine. But where Heidegger's world of function is a world precisely because of the unity of significations that make up the referential totality, Descartes' world of sensibility does not have this unity. The self bathes in sensations, lives its passions, and, as we shall see, can achieve self-esteem by directing and controlling this otherwise disordered existence. To cast Descartes into the systematic framework of Heidegger, we might say that Heidegger's world of function is already a departure from the sensuous life that Descartes characterizes.

This means that beneath Heidegger's "world" lies a subterranean existence, the life of the body, that Heidegger's analysis fails to recognize. Thus, when Levinas begins his analysis of consciousness by casting his gaze to sensuality, he is departing from Heidegger and turning towards Descartes. Prior to the entry into Husserl's world of the phenomenological reduction, and prior still to Heidegger's world of technique, unfolds yet another domain of meaning, not one based in any organized totality or system, but one based on the chaos of sensuous life as it is lived. The priority of this passive mode of existence distinguishes Descartes from Heidegger. It will also distinguish Levinas from Husserl and Heidegger. If it were not for this passive moment, there could be no possibility of an active response, for it is precisely this passive moment, this passion, that provides the impetus to direct thought—whether theoretical (as in Husserl) or technical (as in Heidegger)—in a particular direction.

Descartes indicates that the passions of the soul are modes of understanding life on a passive level, and Levinas follows him, noting that over and against the intentionality of reason lies a non-representational and affective variety of intentionality that is to be characterized not by an active posture of constituting meaning, but by a receptive mode of finding it incumbent on me. Passive receptivity does not merely provide the matter out of which the world is forged. The passions are not empty, vacuous thoughts, but vehicles of meaning for governing practical life.

From Passion to Moral Autonomy

Descartes believes that the passions are necessary for practical life. They provide qualitative "information" about our relationship to things and other people. They instruct us as to what is beneficial and harmful for the mind-body composite. But unrestrained, they can also lead to the worst of harm, because the passions tend to exaggerate. " . . . [T]he passions almost always cause the goods they represent, as well as the evils, to appear much greater and more important than they are, thus moving us to pursue the former and flee from the latter with more ardour and zeal than is appropriate" (*PWD* I 377). Apparently, if one wishes to use the passions to their full benefit, she must take control over them and direct them appropriately. Otherwise, she is tossed about by her passions, made subject to the whims of "animal spirits" and is, consequently, not free. Instead, she lives life as an animal, determined solely by her environment.[12] Thus, Descartes writes that "the chief use of wisdom lies in its teaching us to be masters of our passions and to control them with such skill that the evils which they cause are quite bearable, and even become a source of joy" (*PWD* I 404). Earlier in the same work, Descartes indicates that every human being has this ability: "[t]here is no soul so weak that it cannot, if well-directed, acquire an absolute power over its passions" (*PWD* I 348).

Since the will can control the passions, the will and the passions are not identical. Furthermore, if the "whole" human being is both body and mind, as Descartes told Gassendi, then the "whole" human being integrates these two varieties of thought. Integration, in this case, cannot simply be a matter of the will repressing the passions. The "inclinations of the will" belong to the first primitive notion and, hence, to the *ego cogito*. Yet, Descartes indicated to Gassendi that the "whole man" is not the *ego cogito* in isolation. Somehow, then, the whole human being includes the passions.

The passions, however, unfold under the auspices of the third primitive notion. As opposed to the active *ego cogito*, here the self is defined by its receptivity. In passion, the self is the patient of someone's or something's activity. Passions are "confused thoughts, which the mind does not derive from itself alone but experiences as a result of something happening to the body with which it is closely conjoined" (*PWD* I 281). So, in order for the will to control the passions, the self of the first primitive notion, the *ego cogito*, must act on the self of the third primitive notion, the self defined by its receptivity. This is tantamount to having the active self act on the passive self, or in simpler terms, it is a matter of the self affecting itself, being both the agent and patient of its own activity. Integration of the parts into the "whole man" must, therefore, be a matter of the self overcoming its passion, the active self overcoming the passive.

One important effect of self-overcoming is that in freeing himself from the throes of passion, the human being is liberated from the causal determination of his environment. Mastering self-control is a matter of becoming free to determine one's own action. So, self-overcoming means becoming autonomous, redefining oneself as agent instead of patient. The active self in isolation, the *ego cogito* considered under the auspices of the first primitive notion, is free from the determination of its environment, since it is only the active component of the self. Yet, the *ego cogito* is not free in the same sense as the autonomous whole man who has mastered his passions without denying them. The former is hypothetically free since it unfolds only in the realm of pure intellection; the latter is concretely and practically free since it unfolds in lived experience. The former has no passion, the latter is influenced by passion without being controlled by it.

The significant difference between these two varieties of freedom becomes apparent in Descartes' characterization of the self who has overcome her passions. This is the generous soul; it is also the one with self-esteem. We will see shortly that the only way one can become whole is to become moral, which is a matter of becoming free in the practical sense. Thus, while it might be true that the *ego cogito* is autonomous in a preferential sense—that is, it can choose between thinking about triangles or rectangles—it is not autonomous in the deeper, moral sense. Moral autonomy, unlike preferential autonomy, is not only a matter of knowing the difference between right and wrong, but also of having a strong commitment to doing what is right. This is to say that moral autonomy unfolds as *an obligated freedom* and not as the pure freedom of the *ego cogito*. The only way to find freedom in the practical sphere is to commit oneself to virtue and be good. For Descartes, it is also the only way to find self-esteem.

So far, I have put my conclusions ahead of the evidence. This is because Descartes does not lay out these claims explicitly in the moral language that I have adopted here. His claims on morals are fragmentary. In fact, he wrote to Chanut that "normally I refuse to write down my thoughts concerning morality" (*PWD* III 326). Instead, his opinions on morality come to us as scattered words of advice to friends and passing references to the virtues and how they are acquired. Nowhere does he provide a complete and systematic treatise on morality. For this reason, he is not always clear on the details, particularly when explaining how one concept (such as self-esteem) is linked to another (like generosity). In what follows, I will provide a textual exposition on integration and the origins of moral autonomy in Descartes. Where he is unclear, I may be unclear as well.

Though passions are good, for Descartes, they must be controlled if they are not going to lead us astray. We control the passions by using the active will to overcome them. This control, therefore, grants us independence from the passions and makes us self-determined. When the soul acts on itself in this way and acquires self-determination, it produces the particular auto-affected passion of self-esteem.

Esteem, a sub-species of wonder, is "the soul's inclination to represent to itself the value of the object of its esteem." It represents objects, though in a mode of value, and it can be directed towards the self (*PWD* I 383). The import of self-esteem is revealed in Descartes' reasons for esteeming oneself. "I see only one thing in us which could give us good reason for esteeming ourselves, namely, the exercise of our free will and the control we have over our volitions. For we can reasonably be praised or blamed only for actions that depend upon this free will. It renders us in a certain way like God by making us masters of ourselves . . . " (*PWD* I 384). Self-esteem arises, then, with self-determination.

Descartes links self-esteem with self-determination because volitional control is the only power that the self actually possesses. He writes that "nothing truly belongs to [man] but this freedom to dispose his volitions, and that he ought to be praised or blamed for no other reason than his using this freedom well or badly" (*PWD* I 384). Other considerations, such as "intelligence, beauty, riches, honours, etc.," do not lead to self-esteem, but to a passion that is a close relative, "a highly blameworthy vanity" (*PWD* I 386). Externals, like beauty and so forth, originate outside of the self, and, hence, cannot contribute to its true value. True self-esteem must originate within the self as the acquisition of self-determination. In another letter to Elizabeth, Descartes implies that the satisfaction of overcoming the passions is directly proportional to the effort needed to overcome them (*PWD* III 263). In the same letter, this satisfaction is directly linked to becoming free from one's passions. If by "satisfaction" Descartes means something like self-esteem—the letter equates satisfaction with happiness with oneself—then certainly only the being with passions can experience such esteem. If there is nothing to overcome, there can be no satisfaction in overcoming it. Thus, the will taken in isolation as the *ego cogito* considered under the first primitive notion is incapable of self-esteem. Shortly, we will see that this also renders it incapable of generosity.

The satisfaction of self-esteem arises from self-overcoming. At first this might seem to suggest that self-esteem is an egoistic affair. Being emancipated from the passions—thereby, becoming autonomous—would seem to have no bearing on morality. But where the *ego cogito* in isolation is capable only of preferential autonomy, the self that has overcome the passions has earned the right to be called morally autonomous. This is because "generosity . . . causes a person's self-esteem to be as great as it may legitimately be" (*PWD* I 384). Perfect self-esteem is inseparable from perfect generosity.

Admittedly, Descartes is unclear about how self-esteem and generosity are precisely linked. Nonetheless, he thinks they are intimately tied. Some type of reasoning in anticipation of Kant seems to have its play behind the scenes. Since self-esteem indicates a self considered in its truest moral character as self-determination, it also contains the realization that the human essence is simply self-determination. So, self-esteem converts naturally into humility. Descartes writes that "[w]e have humility as a virtue when . . . we do not prefer ourselves to anyone else and we think that since others have free will just as much as we do, they may use it just as well as we use ours" (*PWD* I 385). Self-esteem includes the recognition that the same power that makes me worthy of esteem makes all free beings worthy of the same. Likewise, Kant will argue that because there is no reason to prefer the self to the other where morals are concerned, the good will is committed to the ends of others just as much as it is to its own. This would naturally make it generous.

An analysis of generosity in Descartes seems to suggest that generosity as the perfection of self-esteem is precisely the extension of self-esteem to the esteem of the other following these Kantian-style guidelines. Generosity is resolvable into two components:

> The first consists in [a person's] knowing that nothing truly belongs to him but this freedom to dispose his volitions, and that he ought to be praised or blamed for no other reason than his using this freedom well or badly. The second consists in his feeling within himself a firm and constant resolution to use it well—that is, never to lack the will to undertake and carry

out whatever he judges to be best. To do that is to pursue virtue in a perfect manner. (*PWD* I 384)

The second component, the resolution to use the will well, coupled with the
recognition that human beings are fundamentally their power of self-determination, leads to esteem of the other. Descartes writes, "Those who possess
this knowledge and this feeling about themselves readily come to believe that
any other person can have the same knowledge and feeling about himself,
because this involves nothing which depends on someone else. That is why
such people never have contempt for anyone" (*PWD* I 384). Those who have
perfect self-esteem also esteem others.

Self-esteem is the result of a strong will. But this is not to say that self-
esteem emerges from a good will, unless self-esteem converts naturally to
esteem of others, to generosity. Yet, it is generosity which "causes a person's
self-esteem to be as great as it may legitimately be" (*PWD* I 384). The circle
is apparent and is repeated in related texts. Descartes suggests that generosity
is "the volition we feel within ourselves to make good use of our free will"
(*PWD* I 386). It is, therefore, something more than self-esteem. But as the
passage continues, he opposes generosity to illegitimate causes of self-esteem, thereby suggesting that generosity causes self-esteem and not self-
esteem generosity. I am uncertain how this difficulty might be resolved. One
suggestion might be to take self-esteem and generosity to be two sides of the
same coin, two components of the same movement towards autonomy. However they relate in the details of their intimacy, it is certainly clear that Descartes sees no way to take them apart from each other. They are mutually
defined in such a way that the perfection of self-esteem as self-determination
is unable to occur without generosity. So, the independence that unites the
active and passive selves in a gesture of self-overcoming leads to freedom,
to be sure, but to an obligated freedom, unlike the freedom of preferential
autonomy.

This is particularly apparent when we consider Descartes' two-fold characterization of the components of generosity. Moral autonomy, I noted earlier,
differs from preferential autonomy in that the former consists of an ability
to tell right from wrong *and* to have a firm commitment to do what is right,

whereas the latter is simply the freedom to choose. Descartes captures the essence of moral autonomy when he writes that generosity consists also "in his feeling within himself a firm and constant resolution to use [the will] well" (*PWD* I 384). This resolution is nothing other than the conversion of a possible preference—to use the will well—from the status of a desire to an ought. Generosity, which is intimately tied to self-esteem and self-determination, is also intimately tied to self-control. In fact, Descartes notes that "[t]hose who are generous . . . have complete command over their passions" (*PWD* I 385). In turn, this means that the integration of will and passion (mind and body) unfolds as moral autonomy, as an obligated freedom, unlike the freedom of the *ego cogito* in isolation.

In the previous chapter, I indicated the problems for practical philosophy that arose when the world was reduced to pure thought. I also showed how Heidegger tried to recover the practical world by appealing to function as Dasein's primary mode of Being-in-the-world. The present chapter began with sensibility to establish a more primordial level of life than either function or theory. For Descartes, prior to the phenomenological reduction (the act of withdrawing the mind from the senses) the integrated human being dwells in a practical world animated by passion under the control of the will in some type of moral order. (This is not to say that practical life is necessarily moral, only that it unfolds under the auspices of an obligation to use the will correctly. It unfolds in an order where morals are an issue.) The turn towards function issues out of a desire to improve this practical order; it is not synonymous with it. Concrete life is prior to both theory and practice, even if I live from theory and practice. In the next chapter, I will trace the terrain covered here through the work of Emmanuel Levinas. Though Levinas fits nicely into the Cartesian structures laid out in the current chapter, he also goes beyond them by explaining how self-determination is obligated and, consequently, how freedom becomes moral autonomy. In the final chapter, I will follow Levinas' style of analysis and attempt to elucidate the existential connection between self-esteem and generosity.

Chapter Three

Levinas Beyond the Horizons of Cartesianism

Before beginning this exposition of Levinas' work, I need to address an important change of position between Levinas' *Totality and Infinity*, written in 1961, and his *Otherwise than Being or Beyond Essence*, written in 1974. In the first work, the self is exposed to the extra-mental in general before another person comes on the scene. In *Otherwise than Being*, the other person is the first to appear, before any exposure to the extra-mental in general. This difference—which might, at first, appear to be insignificant—is important because it affects the analysis of the self and its relationship to the other.

In *Totality and Infinity*, the self bathes in sensibility under the rubric of enjoyment. Enjoyment is further characterized by its affective character: "[w]hat is termed an affective state does not have the dull monotony of a state, but is a vibrant exaltation in which dawns the self. For the I is not the *support* of enjoyment. The 'intentional' structure is here wholly different; the I is the very contraction of sentiment . . . " (*TI* 118). In enjoyment, the self is constituted by an affective intentionality; this is different from the representational intentionality that characterizes the *ego cogito*. Yet, like the *ego cogito*, the self of enjoyment is *self*-centered or egoistic. When the other person comes on the scene, she calls this egoism into question and ethics is born. Ethics, for Levinas, emerges precisely as a contestation of my egoistic tendency to possess the other. Since the other person calls this egoism into question and is revealed as other precisely in doing so, the egoistic self must be established beforehand. In other words, enjoyment is a necessary condition for the revelation of the other person.

Before the other person appears, however, the self is exposed to some kind of alterity (otherness). Levinas writes:

> The intentionality of enjoyment can be described by contrast with the intentionality of representation; it consists in holding on to the exteriority which the transcendental method involved in representation suspends. To hold on to exteriority is not

simply equivalent to affirming the world, but is to posit oneself in it corporeally. (*TI* 127)

And elsewhere, "To be sure, in the satisfaction of need the alienness of the world that founds me loses its alterity" (*TI* 129). If the world loses its alterity in the satisfaction of a need, it must have had it beforehand. Furthermore, since need defines the self in enjoyment, the world prior to enjoyment is other in some sense, even if it loses this otherness by giving way to the possessive egoism of the self.

Unlike the alterity of the world which gives itself over to the self's possessive tendencies, the alterity of persons surpasses my enjoyment by calling it into question. The other person cannot be reduced to the self. Thus, the alterity of persons and that of things is significantly different. Persons resist possession, things do not. Because of this difference, persons are the types of beings that can be violated, while things are not.

Levinas is not always clear about which meaning of "alterity" he is using. This ambiguity makes several passages in Levinas difficult to decipher. Hiding behind this ambiguity, however, is another, more pressing, one. Levinas notes that subjectivity is born by being exposed to the other. In certain passages, he clearly indicates that subjectivity arises from exposure to a personal other. Yet, he speaks of an egoistic self of enjoyment that is "there" prior to the advent of the other person. Obviously, the egoistic self—also characterized subjectively—must represent a subjectivity of a different order.

In some passages, Levinas speaks of a "subjectivity of being," the self on the level of enjoyment. In other places, he speaks of subjectivity as "the self held hostage by the other." This condition represents an ethical subjectivity, the birth of the moral self. In addition, he speaks of a "rational subjectivity," the *ego cogito* and its related field. While the subject of enjoyment is situated within a world that it possesses in enjoyment and which is revealed only in the satisfaction of a need, the subject of ethics is constantly held in a tension between its tendency to possess the other and the other person's resistance to possession. Indeed, it is precisely the self's desire to possess the other together with the other's refusal to be possessed that reveals the other person *as other*. The difference between personal and non-personal alterity is precisely what delineates ethical subjectivity from the subjectivity of being.

In *Totality and Infinity*, the subjectivity of being precedes ethical subjectivity, which, in turn, precedes rational subjectivity. In *Otherwise than Being*, exposure to the alterity of the world in enjoyment is no longer prior to the approach of the other person. The other person becomes the foundation of all otherness.[1] For the sake of simplicity, I will present this chapter primarily from the perspective of *Totality and Infinity*. This will assist in situating Levinas within the horizons of Cartesianism.

Metaphysics and Ontology

Since, for Levinas, metaphysics unfolds on the level of affectivity and ontology on the level of representation, and since the tradition sees ontology and metaphysics on the same level, it is important to distinguish these terms following Levinas' usage before we examine his connection with Descartes. This distinction allows Levinas to use affectivity as a means of transcending the phenomenal world and moving toward the other. Metaphysics, in its deepest sense, is a movement, and not a representation. But, the history of philosophy since Aristotle has taken metaphysics as a branch of inquiry. It has placed ontology within metaphysics, taking both as a science of being. Levinas departs from this tradition, noting that ontology is already bound by representation. He sees, for instance, a theory of being in Husserl's phenomenology, even though Husserl has no recourse to extra-mental "things." This suggests that ontology is too late to capture the original meaning of metaphysics. Levinas writes:

> 'The true life is absent.' But we are in the world. Metaphysics arises and is maintained in this alibi. It is turned toward the 'elsewhere' and the 'otherwise' and the 'other.' For in the most general form it has assumed in the history of thought it appears as a movement going forth from a world that is familiar to us, whatever be the yet unknown lands that bounds it or that it hides from view, from an 'at home' which we inhabit, towards an alien outside-of-oneself, towards a yonder. (*TI* 33)

Metaphysics, in its original manifestation, is a movement, a departure from the known to the unknown, from the self to the other. Aristotle seems to capture this motive element in his *Metaphysics* when he writes that "[a]ll men by nature desire to know. An indication of this is the delight we take in our senses."[2] Philosophy begins not with knowledge, but with curiosity, a desire to know. Furthermore, this desire signals a lack of knowledge. Aristotle, goes on to note, however, that the senses can only give us an acquaintance with particular things; they do not inform us why such-and-such is the case. This role is assigned to wisdom, the fulfillment of the desire to know. So, even though we begin "by wondering that things are as they are . . . we must end in the contrary and, according to the proverb, the better state . . . " (*Meta.* 693). For Aristotle, the attainment of wisdom is better than the desire to know. But it has a price, for fulfilling a desire means the end of that desire. In effect, wisdom, taken here as the attainment of the reason why such-and-such is the case, is parasitic on desire. For Aristotle, clearly it is better to know than to suffer the poverty of not knowing.

Ontology, for Aristotle, follows the lines of rational inquiry. It is the *fulfillment* of the desire to know. It determines what kinds of things there are. Thus, while ontological questioning might begin metaphysically—it carries us from the known to the unknown—attaining a knowledge of being, that is, arriving at an ontology, no longer qualifies as metaphysics in Levinas' terms. It ends by inscribing the unknown in the known thereby foreclosing on transcendence. Arriving at the truth, taken as the result of representation, is the enemy of metaphysical transcendence. If we grant that transcendence is the foundation of all relationships with the other, it is only a small step to understanding how reason is parasitic on interpersonal relations. Here, again, we find the motive behind Levinas' critique of representation.

Levinas finds representations limited because they reduce what is essentially other to a "sphere of ownness," to use Husserl's term.[3] This limitation is not itself problematic, unless our primary concern is to understand the meaning of otherness. Levinas is unable to find this meaning in representation for three reasons. First, representations reduce the other to my consciousness and in so doing strip away the character of otherness that I am seeking to understand: "[w]ithout doubt, the finite being that we are cannot in the final account complete the task of knowledge; but in the limit where this task is accomplished, it consists in making the other become the Same" (*EI* 91). Second, representations "objectify" and "thematize" their objects, that is, intentionality conditions the contents of theoretical consciousness or ascribes essences to things in the very act of knowing.[4] Third, representations "totalize" their objects by reducing what is other to a set of horizons in the conceptual field of the self.[5] By reducing experience to representation, I am, in effect, reducing it to an interpretation conditioned by my other experiences in an effort to have my experience make sense *to me*. This interpretive element of representation means, following Freud, that my representations are autobiographical.

In a sense, each of these reasons is equivalent to the others; this is clear when we recognize that representations arise from an act of constitution. Representational constitution, that act of consciousness whereby the world becomes known, issues out from the subject towards the outside. If representational constitution exhausts consciousness, little room is left for any meaningful content to come to the subject from the outside. Thus, to say that a representation is conditioned presents us with a big problem, if we say that representations are all there is to meaning. Ultimately this means that every act of meaning says more about the subject doing the constituting than it does about the object of the representation. We could, in a leap of faith, maintain that since all rational agents do this in the same way, we all ascribe a similar meaning to the world. (Is this not what Kant maintained?) But, this is mere assertion unless some possibility of contact with the other is opened to the subject whereby the subject can be exposed to what comes from without. Thus, in a sense, Levinas asks Descartes' question; how can representations relate to what is beyond consciousness? Clearly, the answer cannot be found in representational intentionality. For Levinas, it will be found in transcendence, that prior movement towards the outside that animates reason, even if reason succeeds by denying this transcendence. He writes, "The possibility of representing to oneself and the resultant temptation to idealism do indeed profit already from the metaphysical relation and the relationship with the absolutely other, but they attest separation in the midst of this very transcendence" (*TI* 123). Indeed, reason itself is already a response to the other, hence, an indication of the other. In Aristotle's language, it is the *desire* to know that attests to the other, not the resulting knowledge. Thus, once Levinas has found an access to alterity, he will be able to salvage reason from the claim that reason cannot give us an access to the other person. Here metaphysics enters the picture.

"Ontology," etymologically and in practice, speaks of a "science of being." If it is the case that representations cannot give us a picture of what is other, with regard to either persons or things, then ontology cannot be a study of what lies beyond consciousness. Hence, Levinas notes a fundamental difference between "ontology" and "metaphysics." He writes, "The relation with Being that is enacted as ontology consists in neutralizing the existent in order to comprehend or grasp it. It is hence not a relation with the other as such but the reduction of the other to the same" (*TI* 45-46). "Metaphysics," on the other hand, provides the basis for the acts of knowing that make up ontology through a relation with an existent, and "this relation with an *existent* . . . precedes all ontology; it is the ultimate relation in Being. Ontology presupposes metaphysics" (*TI* 48). Consequently, a relation with other persons arises before the constitution of a world. Levinas characterizes this relationship by its passivity, opposing it to the constituting powers of reason, which are active. The relationship with the other lies in "being affected by" him, in passion.

Having separated metaphysics from ontology, it is now possible to understand what Levinas means by titling his last major work, *Otherwise than Being or Beyond Essence*. Why would one who seeks contact with what is radically other attempt to get beyond being? The answer to this question lies again in the characterization of knowledge as representational. As I mentioned above, Levinas is not entirely an anti-rationalist, and on many points he follows his teacher, Husserl. For example, there is only one world for Levinas, the constituted world. To predicate a world behind the constituted world is to make a critical mistake, for this involves predicating what is found in consciousness and thematized in representations to what is extra-mental. In a sense, such a predication must involve a denial of the thematizing character of representations. Behind such representations, Levinas finds only the element, the place where one bathes in sensibility. It is not a world, because, for him, world implies order, and order reason.

Likewise, terms associated with ontology (and here Levinas includes "being") are already thematized by consciousness. Hence, predicating "being" to what is beyond consciousness commits the same error.[6] In sensibility and in metaphysical relationship "being" does not present itself as a category. Thus, the metaphysical relation is not a relation with being, but a relation with something beyond being, or beyond consciousness. "Alterity figures in [the beyond] outside any qualification of the other for the ontological order and outside any attribute" (*OBBE* 16).

To reach this "beyond" Levinas will have to disengage himself from traditional ontological and epistemic categories.[7] Thus, Levinas departs from traditional means of expression and presents his discourse in evocative terms. Herein lies not only the obscurity of his texts, but also the foundations for his metaphysics of affectivity.

Levinas and Descartes

Already several similarities between Levinas and Descartes suggest themselves. Both thinkers characterize the self as multi-dimensional, separating the active and rational *ego cogito*, that is, rational subjectivity, from a passive self grounded in sensibility. Furthermore, both seem to agree that the moral human being, what I have here defined as ethical subjectivity, is neither rational subjectivity nor the passive subjectivity of being taken in isolation, though both of these modes of subjectivity are necessary, in some way or another, for ethical subjectivity to emerge.

Since Levinas characterizes the other on a theological model, noting that the other person is also at the same time a revelation of the absolute other, or God, even the change of position between *Totality and Infinity* and *Otherwise than Being* suggests a Cartesian motif. It is reminiscent of Descartes' Third Meditation, where the idea of God is found already implanted within rational subjectivity and is, therefore, discovered after the *ego cogito*. Yet, after careful analysis the idea of God turns out to be prior to the idea of the self. In the order of investigation, the self must come first, but in the order of metaphysical priority, God is prior to the self as the ontological possibility of the self.

There can be no doubt that Levinas is aware of his debt to Descartes. He explicitly notes the inversion of priorities that situates the idea of God before the idea of the self. "The ambiguity of Descartes's first evidence, revealing the I and God in turn without merging them, revealing them as two distinct moments of evidence mutually founding one another, characterizes the very meaning of separation" (*TI* 48). Separation, for Levinas, is what permits the recognition of the other as other. On other fronts as well, Levinas is profoundly Cartesian. Most notably, he uses Descartes' discovery that the idea of infinity cannot be derived from rational subjectivity and, therefore, signals an idea that must have been put in him by God. Levinas takes this to mean that rational subjectivity is already penetrated by the other. Because the idea of God is prior to the idea of the self, Levinas remarks that exposure to the other is the metaphysical condition that gives rise to the self. Without the other, there could be no self-awareness.

Secondly, though no less importantly, Levinas praises Descartes' doctrine of sensibility. He writes that "[t]he profundity of the Cartesian philosophy of the sensible consists . . . in affirming the irrational character of sensation, an idea forever without clarity and distinctness, belonging to the order of the useful and not of the true" (*TI* 135). Here, Levinas reveals his respect for Descartes' characterization of the "third primitive notion" as an element of human understanding beyond representation. The "third primitive notion," as the reader will recall, is the seat of passion for Descartes; furthermore, it is the level on which mind and body are "understood" as a unity. Sensibility is not of the order of reason; and Levinas, like Descartes, places affectivity on the level of sensibility. This means that affectivity, like sensibility, is not of the order of reason. But this simple correlation between Levinas and Descartes is not sufficient to warrant approaching Levinas from Descartes particularly, since many thinkers have noted that affectivity is not of the order of reason and even that affectivity is prior to reason. We need, then, to look at the relationship between Descartes and Levinas more closely.

In Chapter Two, I noted that Descartes requires affectivity to reveal the complete metaphysical significance of the self as an integrated and whole being. Once the ego is affected it can realize the meaning of generosity, its being for the other. In Levinas we find the same theme. Through affectivity, a human being is separated from pure thought through what Levinas calls a "refusal of the concept." Levinas writes that "[t]his refusal of the concept drives the being that refuses it into the dimension of interiority. It is at home with itself" (*TI* 118). The affective dawning of a self as independent, hence, separate, makes possible the recognition of the other person as an *other* not dependent on me. Generosity now becomes an indication of the presence of the other person to me. Levinas writes:

> It is in generosity that the world possessed by me—the world open to en-joyment—is apperceived from a point of view independent of the egoist position. The "objective" is not simply the object of an impassive contem-plation. Or rather impassive contemplation is defined by gift, by the aboli-tion of inalienable property. The presence of the Other is equivalent to this calling into question of my joyous possession of the world. (*TI* 75-76)

This "calling into question" reveals a self that initially possessed the world, a self that is now separated from its world through affectivity, not through reason. Levinas remarks that "[w]hen the I is identified with reason, taken as the power of thematization and objectification, it looses its very ipseity" (*TI* 119). We might say, quite literally, that when the self is identified with the *ego cogito*, it de-materializes. Thus, the material self that is capable of possessing the world, the ego that is the very possibility of possessing the world in representational intentionality, is "realized" in an affective moment "beneath" representations. This "affective moment" is called "enjoyment," through which the self separates from its environment and becomes a subject unto itself. All of this arises simply from *having* sensations.

Thus, affectivity, construed here as separation and enjoyment, is necessary for a relation with the alterity of the other person, because such a relation requires two persons who are not assimilated into each other; generosity preserves this "space" between self and other allowing the self to emerge as independent of the other. On this point, as well, we find Levinas within a Cartesian framework, for it was Descartes who indicated that independence and generosity were correlative. Furthermore, Levinas writes, "There is in knowledge, in the final account, an impossibility of escaping the self; hence sociality cannot have the same structure as knowledge" (*EI* 60). Similarly, Descartes writes, "[I]t is the ordinary course of life and conversation, and abstention from meditation and from the study of things which exercise the imagination, that teaches us how to conceive the union of the soul and the body" (*PWD* III 227).

If the reader has granted the conclusion from Chapter Two that once the mind is incarnated in the body, the subject is situated within the practical world, and if it is further accepted that incarnation unfolds in social interaction—as the quote suggests, namely through the ordinary course of life and conversation, and abstaining from meditation—then Levinas' statement above rings with Cartesian overtones. Descartes explicitly mentions "conversation," a notion that Levinas will use to bridge the gap between one person and another.

Furthermore, both thinkers assign a similar function to the affects in relating the mind to the body. Affections, for Descartes, incarnate the mind in the body. Levinas writes that the body is not "an object among other objects" but "the very regime in which separation holds sway . . . " (*TI* 163). Elsewhere he writes, "'Incarnate thought' is not initially produced as a thought that acts on the world, but as a separated existence which affirms its independence . . . " (*TI* 164-165). In addition, Lingis points out, speaking on Levinas' behalf, "It is in the incarnation of consciousness that subjectivity is exposed to the exterior and committed to alterity" (*OBBE* xxix). So, Levinas and Descartes both differentiate between two levels of human existence, the rational and the sensual. More importantly, both see the affective dimension intimately related to the possibility of social interaction and, therefore, to the possibility of relating to another being that exists beyond my consciousness.

Another important parallel concerns a recognition on the part of both thinkers that, though idealism is a temptation and does have philosophical merit, by itself it is destined to lead to problems. For instance, in *The Theory of Intuition in Husserl's Phenomenology*, Levinas levels the charge of "intellectualism" against Husserl for thinking that there was only one type of intentionality, that is, representational intentionality (*TIHP* 94). The problem with asserting that all human understanding—construed here in its broadest possible sense to include both feeling and thought—arises from representations is that if all human understanding is representational, then we are left with no recourse to anything above and beyond representations whereby ideas can be called representations at all. Without presence, re-*presentation* is impossible, or representation yields truth only by re-placing presence, leading to idealism. Both Levinas and Descartes resist idealism by allowing sensibility a legitimate place in human existence. Both thinkers characterize knowledge as idealistic, but both concede that there is more to human existence than knowing. Levinas, for instance, goes beyond his predecessors, observing that to "comprehend" an object in a representation is to strip the alterity from something that is initially other by setting it within the horizons of the self's thought, or, as he says explicitly, a representation is "a determination of the other by the same, without the same being determined by the other" (*TI* 170). This simple shift from "other" to "same" is sufficient to alter the fundamental characteristic of what is other, namely, its otherness. Once "otherness" is stripped from the other by representation, the other is constituted by my consciousness and, therefore, belongs to it. The original relationship between self and other is upset, and the extra-mental other is replaced with a concept. "[R]epresentation claims to substitute itself *after the event* for this life in reality, so as to constitute this very reality" (*TI* 169). It arises only *after* sensual experience, though prior to the experience of objects. This process of reducing sensuous life to representation is analogous to the act of withdrawing the mind from the senses that Descartes undertakes with the dream argument discussed in Chapter One. Like Levinas, he notes that the act of retreating into the interiority of pure thought at the same time redefines the referent of outer perception as an idea within his mind.

Forgetting this reductive character of thought means entering into idealism, since once the ideal is affirmed as the real, sensual experience, by onto-

logical necessity, is defined as un-real. Any meaning that arises from a relationship between the self and the extra-mental other also suffers demotion in
the same gesture. Thus, to reduce experience to the real (i.e., ideal) and to
define this domain as the "true" world is, at the same time, to renounce the
affective sub-structures that enable all relationships with extra-mental others.
That Levinas has recourse to the event as it is "lived through" prior to all
knowledge will save him from being an idealist himself. This access to
human experience as it is "lived through" must of necessity be non-representational since it will be the condition for all representation. It is found in
sensibility which is, for Levinas, "not to be confused with still vacillating
forms of 'consciousness of.' It is not separated from thought by a simple
difference of degree, not even by a difference in the nobility or the extent of
expansion of their objects" (*TI* 137). Instead, sensibility becomes the possibility of representation. It is "prior to reason; the sensible is not to be as-
cribed to the totality to which it is closed" (*TI* 138). When Descartes characterizes the entry into pure reason as a "withdrawal from the senses," he is,
in effect, making the same claim. The entry into reason leaves sensibility
behind.

To be sure, Levinas carries his analysis of sensibility further than Descartes, noting that to sense is "to enjoy, to refuse the unconscious prolonga-
tions, to be thoughtless, that is, without ulterior motives . . . " (*TI* 139) and
that "[t]he separation accomplished as enjoyment, that is, as interiority, becomes a consciousness of objects" (*TI* 139). He does more with sensibility
than Descartes. Nonetheless, the two agree on some fundamental differences
between reason and sensibility. Each thinker gives each mode of being its
due, recognizing that sociality and sensuality are, somehow, correlative as are
solipsism and rationality. This agreement and the subsequent tendency to see
reason as a departure from the senses that alters the very meaning of sensuous experience is sufficient to situate Levinas within a Cartesian perspective.

Sensibility, Separation, and Subjectivity

Like Descartes, Levinas analyzes sensibility at a point before thought originates, before representational intentionality has its play in making sense out of sensation and ordering the world. This endows sensibility with its metaphysical employment. If we are to understand sensation as something that is non-representational, it is vital that we do not confuse sensation with perception. Perceptions are representations, sensation of the third grade for Descartes. On this level, the ego has already constituted an object, situating it within the world. These perceptions are already thematized by the intellect. Sensations, on the other hand, are somewhat chaotic. They do not reveal objects, but a rush of disordered sensations. Here, Levinas agrees with Descartes' sentiment that "bodies are not strictly speaking perceived by the senses at all, but only by the intellect" (*PWD* II 95). But if sensations are part of the link that orients the self towards the other, then on some level of consciousness, we must possess both sensation and some mode of being aware of sensation that is non-representational. For Descartes, this meant that sensations were both thoughts and physical reactions. Sensation was not an act of the *ego cogito*, but of the mind-body composite. Furthermore, it was revealed in receptivity, in being susceptible to the passions.

Levinas concurs, though he takes his analysis in a slightly different direction, opposing himself to Husserl, who also recognized that sensibility has two components, sensation and an awareness of the same. Richard Cohen notes, "Despite the intentional closure within which phenomenological analysis hoped to operate, Husserl always got into difficulties when he examined sensations. Whatever sensations are, they appear to participate in, yet overflow, the active syntheses of representational consciousness."[8] This "overflow" of sensations indicates that even after the act of representation there seems to be some residue of sensation that remains unrepresented. (This, in turn, implies an awareness of the overflow.) Such overflow raises serious problems for Husserl, because sensations are "meant to be foundational, in Husserl's terms, 'absolute.' And yet Husserl himself admits that sensations seem somehow to exceed the unification effected by passive-synthesis" (Cohen 198). Keeping in mind that "passive synthesis" involves a synthesis of perceptual consciousness, the observation that sensation somehow overflows passive synthesis means that there is a point where what is "beyond consciousness" is opened to the subject beyond representation.

At the same time, however, a door through which sensations can flow is a violation of Husserl's epoché; if his phenomenology takes him to a point where he must acknowledge the real existence of data *coming from without,* then he has not, in fact, successfully bracketed the question of the ontic reality of everything "beyond consciousness." While this is not problematic for Levinas—it, in fact, opens up an access to the other—it is problematic for Husserl, whose method requires the full use of the epoché in order to get his project off the ground.

Noting Husserl's intellectualism, Levinas analyzes this overflow of sensation (that element of sensation that remains un-represented) under the rubric of happiness and enjoyment, or under the broader category of affectivity. This, in turn, carries Levinas beyond phenomenology. Cohen indicates, "Levinas' notion of happiness [is] based on a radical appropriation and interpretation of the overflow of sensations Husserl noted, and thereby a notion which goes beyond passive-synthesis and thus beyond phenomenology proper" (Cohen, 198). Going beyond phenomenology is important here, for in going beyond phenomena, to a point before a particular phenomenon is constituted, we can reach otherness without reducing it to a representation. This is to *encounter* otherness as it is in itself *as other.* The meaning found in this encounter is not representational, for Levinas, but affective. He pushes his theory as far as theory can go, to affectivity. From here, however, affectivity must reveal its own meaning apart from representation. The other person is then to be "understood" not as an ontological entity, but as the ethical other. The other will not be revealed in the content of a thought, but precisely in my obligation as the one to whom I am obligated.

To get to the point where we can go beyond phenomenology proper, it is important to understand that sensation is related to both perception and affectivity, as it was for Descartes earlier. "[T]he sensation graspable by introspection is already a perception" (*TI* 187), writes Levinas, where perception presents thematized qualities of objects. "[C]olor is always extended and objective, the color of a dress, a lawn, a wall; sound is a noise of a passing car, or a voice of someone speaking" (*TI* 187). But life as it is lived, rather than understood in representation, is lived precisely as enjoyment, the satisfaction of being "full" with sensations, the satisfaction of "living from" the environment, encountering things as "nourishments." Recognizing enjoyment as a characteristic of lived experience provides access to the affective dimensions of sensation. Levinas writes:

> Enjoyment, by essence satisfied, characterizes all sensations whose representational content dissolves into their affective content. The very distinction between representational and affective content is tantamount to a recognition that enjoyment is endowed with a dynamism other than that of perception. (*TI* 187)

Sensations are not, then, for Levinas, mere "contents destined to fill a priori forms of objectivity" (*TI* 188). Rather,

> The notion of sensation is thus somewhat rehabilitated. In other words, sensation recovers a "reality" when we see in it not the subjective counterpart of objective qualities, but an enjoyment "anterior" to the crystallization of consciousness, I and non-I, into subject and object. (*TI* 188)

The reality recovered in sensation provides our access to the other person as an other "beyond consciousness." But, before proceeding to how Levinas envisions this exposure to the other person, we must undertake a further analysis of enjoyment to show how sensibility as an affective mode of understanding gives rise to separation and subjectivity. We must examine what enjoyment accomplishes.

Levinas notes that we "live from" our environment and our activity within that environment. "We live from 'good soup,' air, light, spectacles, work, ideas, sleep, etc. . . . These are not objects of representations" (*TI* 110). Levinas does not mean to suggest that these things cannot be represented; rather, he is suggesting that in living from such things we relate to them other than through representations. "To live from" and "to think about" are not the same, though Levinas would want to say that we live also from thinking.

> To live from bread is . . . neither to represent bread to oneself nor to act on it nor to act by means of it. To be sure, it is necessary to earn one's bread, and it is necessary to nourish oneself in order to earn one's bread; thus the bread I eat is also that with which I earn my bread and my life. But if I eat my bread in order to labor and to live, I live *from* my labor and *from* my bread. (*TI* 111)

Departing from Heidegger, who maintains that we live from these things through their functions as tools and implements, Levinas maintains that we live from these things through nourishment. I eat my bread; in the activity of eating it becomes a part of my body. I bathe in the music of Beethoven's "Moonlight Sonata"; in the activity of bathing I digest the music. I am saturated with what I live from.

> Nourishment, as a means of invigoration, is the transmutation of the other into the same, which is in the essence of enjoyment: an energy that is other, recognized as other, recognized, we will see, as sustaining the very act that is directed upon it, becomes, in enjoyment, my own energy, my strength, me. (*TI* 111)

Taking on what nourishes me conveys a separation between me and what has yet to nourish me. "Enjoyment is made of the memory of its thirst; it is a quenching" (*TI* 113). It involves stepping back from my environment; "living from . . . delineates independence itself, the independence of enjoyment and of its happiness . . . " (*TI* 110). Enjoyment is independence precisely because it evinces a separation between the act of living from something and that from which one lives. Before enjoyment, there is me and an other thing that has yet to nourish me, though none of this is revealed until after this need is satisfied. The pain of hunger exhibits itself in separation where my self and the bread that will nourish me are radically independent. I can represent the bread, but this will not feed me. I must eat it. But, this I, which must eat the bread, is already a subject of its need.

For Levinas, however, the need exhibited here is not just a privation; rather, it is a "happy dependence [that] is capable of satisfaction" (*TI* 115). "The human being thrives on his needs; he is happy for his needs" (*TI* 114). Need arises from enjoyment; in enjoyment the subject is at home with herself, satisfied and happy. But need, nourishment, involves going out into the world, to work, to make the self satisfied again. "[N]eed is the primary movement of the same" (*TI* 116).

If Levinas is correct, then the human being starts first as happy, satisfied with the plenum of sensations. He enjoys them. This enjoyment is independence, the initial formation of the I as something distinguished from what is other than itself. Cohen notes:

> [Sensation] is called "happiness" because at this level of sensibility the subject is entirely self-satisfied, self-complacement, content, sufficient. Instead of syntheses, there are vibrations; instead of unifications, there are pulsations; instead of identifications, there are excitations; rather than an extensive ecstatic self, there are margins of intensities, scattered stupidities, involutions without centers—egoism and solitude without substantial unity: a sensational happiness. . . . This event does not happen *to* subjectivity, this eventfulness, this flux, *is* subjectivity. (Cohen, 201)

This subject, born from enjoyment, is not the subject of a representation, the necessary subject of the *cogito*. It is a mind-body unity unfolding in enjoyment. Thus, the I of enjoyment is the I that takes up the project of living, where taking up this project is living, it is not for the sake of living. "Life is affectivity and sentiment; to live is to enjoy life" (*TI* 115). Even the interruption of a need does not destroy this enjoyment. For Levinas, needs can be satisfied in living from the environment, and living from again implies a separation. I am not my environment. "Enjoyment accomplishes the atheist separation; it deformalizes the notion of separation, which is not a cleavage made in the abstract, but the existence at home with itself of an autochthonous I" (*TI* 115).

The human being, separated from its environment in enjoyment, becomes a subject, an identity, before the powers of constitution are set to work; it is made ready for the approach of what is not possessed. This is the meaning of separation on the level of enjoyment: to recognize myself as not identical with my environment. If I seek otherness, I can find it only by not being identified with it, that is, by discovering it as other than me; and this requires separation. In representational intentionality, however, I am not separated from the object—the object becomes mine; it is reduced to the same.

> If cognition in the form of the objectifying act does not seem to us to be at the level of the metaphysical relation, this is not because the exteriority contemplated as an object, the theme, would withdraw from the subject as fast as the abstractions proceed; on the contrary it does not withdraw enough. (*TI* 109)

Here, then, we see the birth of a subjectivity evinced through separation that is not a rational subjectivity. It is the subject of affectivity: the felt self, the self which lives, breathes, and is excited by its work. "Behind theory and practice there is enjoyment of theory and of practice: the egoism of life" (*TI* 113).

In enjoyment, Levinas finds an intentionality which does not objectify its contents, but relates to them non-representationally. Affective intentionality is able to reach towards alterity because it emerges out of an exposure to alterity. In affectivity, the human person is defined by its exposure to what is beyond itself. Though very different from the *ego cogito*, this subjectivity shares one important similarity with it; both are egoistic, absorbing the alterity of the world into the self. When the other person comes on the scene, she calls this egoism into question, thus giving rise to an awareness of another person as other and to another level of subjectivity.

The Self and the Other Person

Levinas presents a self that bathes in sensibility under the rubric of enjoyment. To bathe in sensibility is to be exposed to some type of otherness, but this otherness is capable of being enjoyed or represented and, as such, is unstable before an egoist self. It gives way to the possessive tendencies of the ego. To preserve the radical autonomy of the other person, Levinas will need to show that somehow the other person is distinctly different from mere things. In so doing, Levinas will discover another level of subjectivity that is, in its very depths, ethical.

The self bathing in sensibility is, in a sense, bound up only in a "present" moment of passing impressions. But, the self that bathes in impressions is a body-consciousness unity and is not solipsistic. Craig Vasey suggests that " . . . Levinas' own idea of intentionality as incarnate and of consciousness as impressional means for him that the ego (the Same) is already and always 'possessed by the non-ego, by otherness, by facticity'."[9] Enjoyment evinces separation; again, "satisfaction is made of the memory of its thirst." Thus, the satisfaction of enjoyment and separation includes a metaphysical awareness of otherness in general before consciousness constitutes the world in terms of subjects and objects. But at this level, what is other is simply food for my nourishment, sensual and elemental qualities that are "there" solely for my potential enjoyment. When the other person comes on the scene, he calls these possessive tendencies into question. This calling into question, this resistance, means, for Levinas, that some power beyond thought is acting upon and against the ego. It is the infinite other acting upon and disrupting the totality that is my world. This explains the significance of the title, *Totality and Infinity*. "Totality" refers to the domain of representations, all that is known or capable of being known. "Infinity," on the other hand, refers to that which is unable to be represented: the other person in her otherness. Infinity, for Levinas, is signaled by the face, which is more than the brute appearance of the face as an object in constituted experience. The face *stands for* the *other* person.

The very idea of infinity finds its source for Levinas, as it does for Descartes, in something that cannot be generated from within subjectivity. Levinas writes:

> In what concerns knowledge: it is by essence a relation with what one equals and includes, with that whose alterity one suspends, with what becomes immanent, because it is to my measure and to my scale. I think of Descartes, who said that the *cogito* can give itself the sun and sky; the only thing it cannot give itself is the idea of the Infinite. (*EI* 60)

Though Levinas is in basic agreement with Descartes here, he will go beyond Descartes, noting that the idea of the infinite, for Descartes, remains on the level of representation. This idea, for Levinas, signals a metaphysical desire for the other person. "In Descartes the idea of the Infinite remains a theoretical idea, a contemplation, a knowledge. For my part, I think that the relation to the Infinite is not a knowledge, but a desire" (*EI* 92).

Metaphysical desire—in my mind the most elegant concept in Levinas—is a longing that cannot be satisfied, a recognition that there is more to reality than what is represented, along with a desire to represent that which cannot be represented. It is the desire for the *otherness* of the other. Since *otherness* is precisely what cannot be possessed, this desire is always unsatisfied. As such, it indicates a longing for the infinite, incomprehensible, unknown. . . . So, the idea of infinity—unfolding as desire—indicates a gravity on the part of the outside and the other that pulls the self outward. Levinas notes, "The metaphysical desire for the absolutely other which animates intellectualism (or the radical empiricism that confides in the teaching of exteriority) deploys its *en-ergy* in the vision of the face, or in the idea of infinity" (*TI* 196).

Thus, the infinite is both present to thought as an idea that exceeds its own content and present to sensibility in the face of the other. As such it signals the other's approach, a contact with an alterity manifested as a desire for union, but a desire that cannot be fulfilled. The other person, on this level of consciousness, remains other. He outstrips the totality of my knowledge, always reminding me both of his presence and of my inability to reduce him to the totality of my rational life. Levinas suggests:

> The idea of infinity, the overflowing of finite thought by its content, effectuates the relation of thought with what exceeds its capacity, with what at each moment it learns without suffering shock. . . . The relation with the face, with the other absolutely other which I can not contain, the other in this sense infinite, is nonetheless my Idea, a commerce. But the relation is maintained without violence, in peace with this absolute alterity. . . . The first revelation of the other, presupposed in all other relations with him, does not consist in grasping him in his negative resistance and in circumventing him by ruse. I do not struggle with a faceless god, but I respond to his expression, to his revelation. (*TI* 197)

The face of the other person, the infinite, and its corollary in the idea of the infinite, are beyond the categories of representational thought, beyond the categories of all ontology, hence, beyond being and essence. But, this is not to say that the epiphany of the face of the other person is a meaningless content; on the contrary, it offers a meaning understood only in affectivity as a felt meaning.

The infinite face of the other person, under the rubric of metaphysical desire, marks the point of departure between a metaphysics of affectivity and ethical responsibility. The very meaning of the face is ethical; hence, for Levinas, the metaphysical access to the other person is already ethical, or, in other words, the very meaning given by incarnate intentionality is the radical meaning of the self and the other person as two entirely separate entities related through desire. This desire, in turn, reveals precisely that the other person is not mine, hence, not mine to do with as I please. But the ethical meaning of the other person is not merely the recognition that the other person is not mine, it is also the recognition that the other requires or demands a response, though these two moments are interrelated.

For Levinas, the human being's fundamental exposure to the immediate presence of something that is not itself is rooted in receptivity as a felt meaning of otherness revealed as an obligation to respond. Ethical affectivity is both the awareness of the other person as the one who "affects" me and this command. Responsibility, as we shall see, is the second movement of ethical affectivity, for response implies something to respond to—here, the advent of the other person.

To present affectivity as an element of the human being is to recognize that lived experience must precede the theoretical. But lived experience is more than just brute experience; it includes its own meaning found in feeling, not in ideas. To live through something is, as I have noted above, to live from something, to live somewhere. Living, therefore, already refers to alterity in some sense or other. To be in an environment and yet not to be synonymous with that environment constitutes the self of enjoyment, the egoist self, the pre-ethical subject. So too, in a more profound sense, the other person—who is not able to be enjoyed or represented—indicates both a breach of rational subjectivity and that the world of lived experience is not entirely under my control. Subjectivity, on this level, includes the awareness that I am not alone. The life world, for Levinas, includes other people. It is the world of faces that pass in and out of my life. In this respect, the life world is social. Thus, to say that lived experience precedes the theoretical is to say that the social precedes the theoretical. It is also to say that the meaning of sociality is found, not in theory, but in affectivity.

Thus, Levinas' metaphysics opens up to philosophy a grounding for a region beyond consciousness under the rubric of affectivity. Though this region is not a world of constituted objects, it nonetheless unfolds with meaning and is endowed with deep significance. Hence, we see the metaphysical component of affectivity, as that which reaches beyond consciousness. More importantly, affectivity, in its ethical manifestation, indicates a plurality of consciousnesses each with its own interpretation of the world. The other person, then, even the meaning of the other person, must be construed on another level of consciousness where a relationship between the self and an other does not result in a total encompassing of both into the same. It is only here that we can find an honest respect for the autonomy of the other person, because recognizing his autonomy is precisely to recognize that he is not mine. How this realization comes about is the topic of the next section.

From Sensibility to the Other Person

Sensibility is exposure to otherness; its meaning is given in a non-representational and affective intentionality. Since it is passive, it is open to the approach of what is other. So far, this has been our theme. But Levinas makes a distinction between the passivity of bathing in the element, that is, the passivity of enjoying mere things, and the passivity of being confronted by other persons. The approach of the other person reveals a passivity more passive than the passivity of pure sensibility. In confrontation with the other person, the self is *exposed*. This exposure carries a weight more dramatic than a simple lack of action. He writes:

> Sensibility is exposedness to the other. Not the passivity of inertia, a persistence in a state of rest or of movement, the capacity to undergo the cause that would bring it out of that state. Exposure as a sensibility is more passive still; it is like an inversion of the *conatus* of *esse,* a having been offered without any holding back, a not finding any protection in any consistency or identity of a state. (*OBBE* 75)

Though bathing in elemental sensible qualities is passive, exposedness to the other person is a passivity of a different order. In exposure, I am under threat; I have no place to hide. Thus, Levinas finds an element of vulnerability in sensibility. "In the having been offered without any holding back, it is as though the sensibility were precisely what all protection and all absence of protection already presuppose: vulnerability itself" (*OBBE* 75). Protection is a reactive maneuver. It presupposes the threat of impending harm and is, therefore, related to an ability to be wounded, to vulnerability. Also related is the emergence of another who is perceived to be able to harm me. Thus, one corollary of vulnerability is the presence of a dominant other, the other person who can hurt me.

A second corollary of vulnerability is that the other is proximate. The intensity of my vulnerability is directly proportional to the proximity of the other. I feel myself more vulnerable in the face-to-face relationship than I do when the other is not immediately present. Levinas explains, "Rather than a nature, earlier than nature, immediacy is this vulnerability, this maternity, this pre-birth or pre-nature in which the sensibility belongs. This proximity is narrower, more constrictive, than contiguity, older than every past present" (*OBBE* 75-76).

Burke describes the initial approach of the other person in terms of astonishment or surprise. In so doing, he also notes the essential element of radical passivity that arises from the other person. "My astonishment seems less an activity of mine, a willful projection or a function of my interests, than the deepest mode of passivity."[10] Vulnerability arises from this surprise. The other invades my solitude. "The passivity of astonishment is to be understood in the etymological sense of surprise, 'super-prendere', to be taken over or taken up, with no hope of return through the power of thought. The face of the Other has invaded my solitude, disturbed the egoism of happiness and lifted me toward what is radically not me" (Burke 198). My response to the other is not sanctioned by vulnerability and astonishment, if such notions are solely related to fear. Yet, my being caught off guard is what reveals the radical autonomy and independence of the other person. The passivity of vulnerability indicates that an other *person* is present, unlike the passivity of enjoyment and sensibility, which indicates only the presence of elemental qualities.

For Levinas, this means that on a very basic level the ego is aware of the difference between persons and things, the former being endowed with a transcendent characteristic while the latter lending itself to possession. Furthermore, Levinas notes that the self, taken in a social sense, becomes a subject in its vulnerability before other subjects. This dawning of the social subject unfolds across several moments, beginning with the passivity I have already mentioned here. Other moments include discourse and face-to-face encounters that indicate a proximate other forcing me into subjection (that is, subjectivity) as a being held responsible both to and for the other. Each moment is intimately tied to the others in a type of dependence that is neither ontological nor epistemic. One would do well to call it a "religious dependence," provided that we take "religious" in its etymological sense to mean a reconnecting.

This dependence is articulated by Levinas as a physics of interpersonal space. I passively sit back bathing in elemental qualities, when an incomprehensible transcendence invades my solitude, forcing me into a deeper level of interiority. Since I am under threat, the other emerges as dominant, the one who can harm me. From here the analysis continues, force acting against force, move and countermove, until the self emerges already implicated in a social relation with the other that is both religious and ethical at its deepest levels. The remainder of this chapter is dedicated to articulating some of the various components of this physics. Since these components are intimately linked in a matrix of force and counter-force, it is difficult to present them in a linear manner. Levinas' descriptions often appear repetitious. One concept is introduced with another that both defines and will be defined by the former. For instance, as we have already seen, vulnerability is, at the same time, presence before one who can harm me. It is a revelation of a dominant other standing over a defenseless self. My vulnerability and the dominance of the other are, therefore, correlative. The method continues by searching for other correlates with the ultimate aim of articulating the connection between self and other meeting face-to-face. The difficulty that Levinas' method presents for us is that we must presuppose concepts up front that will not be clarified until later in order to understand what it is that will ultimately clarify them.

Before getting to the business of exploring some of the details of the face-to-face encounter, a comment situating the following analysis within this text seems in order. In Chapter Two, I explored the difference between reason and sensibility in Descartes. I ended that chapter by examining the "whole person" who, according to Descartes, emerges as such by properly directing the passions. There, I noted that becoming whole was intimately tied to becoming generous and that one could be an integrated self only by being other-directed. I also noted at that point that Descartes did not really explain the connection between the self and its obligations to others, though he certainly had an intuition that somehow a full social self was ethically bound to other people. I promised to pick up that theme in Levinas. However, I have not done so yet, presenting instead the distinction between reason and sensibility for Levinas in order to situate him within Cartesian structures. In what remains of this chapter, I will return to the question of how the social self is ethically bound to the other. In brief, the answer is that the same separation between self and other that allows there to be a social self at all requires a relation between self and other that does not dissolve the difference between self and other. The relationship that meets this criterion is precisely the ethical relation, since it takes the other as not mine, that is, as an end-in-itself. Ethics maintains the space between self and other after separation, thereby allowing the self to emerge as a self in reference to the other without possessing the other. Thus, ethics is the possibility of social interaction.

Meeting the Other Face-to-Face

The other is revealed to me in the epiphany of his face. But the presence of the other person in the face is not a perception, not an object of representational intentionality. Rather, it indicates the presence of the infinite, that which cannot be reduced to a representation: "[t]he other remains infinitely transcendent, infinitely foreign; his face in which his epiphany is produced and which appeals to me breaks with the world that can be common to us, whose virtualities are inscribed in our *nature* and developed by our existence" (*TI* 194). In other words, the face of the other person appears from the "other" side of the world, from the other side of being, or from being's exterior. Since the other person comes from beyond the world, that is, before the ordering of a world through the use of reason, she does not emerge in conceptual knowledge. Rather, she emerges in my desire for the exteriority indicated by her face. This does not mean that the other person is dependent on my desire, only that in my desire the other is revealed. Desire opens a domain beyond totality and the egoism of enjoyment. Levinas writes, "If exteriority consists not in being presented as a theme but in being open to desire, the existence of the separated being which desires exteriority no longer consists in caring for Being. To exist has a meaning in another dimension than that of the perduration of the totality; it can go beyond being" (*TI* 301). This other dimension, as we shall see, is the region from which ethics is born; it is a non-constituted domain of meaning that is opened before the powers of thought are set to work.

Access to this domain of meaning occurs in discourse, though not in the content of the words, that is, in what is *said*, but in the *saying*. The meaning of the content of our words, the said, is a matter of conceptual knowledge, but the meaning of the event of saying is beyond knowledge; it unfolds as greeting or regarding the other, and it is prior to the sound of the other's voice. The face speaks even without uttering a word.[11] The saying reveals the other in discourse because it signals the proximity of the other to the self and not because it is a spoken dialogue—the "word" issues from the face of the other person, even if it is a silent word.

But the "saying" is not limited solely to this metaphorical employment. It is also present in what is said; thus, it is present in spoken language as well. Indeed, the saying is the very possibility of the said. To speak *to* the other person is already to have passed into a region beyond the totality of thought, beyond the categories of being and essence. Discourse does not consist solely of the content of my speech, what I must communicate, but also of my directedness towards the other to whom I communicate. This passage beyond the categories of thought characterizes the saying, lending discourse a metaphysical employment.

The meaning of saying unfolds in the affective interplay *between* interlocutors. This differentiates the modes of meaning attributed to the saying and the said.

> . . . the *saying* is the fact that before the face I do not simply remain there contemplating it, I respond to it. The saying is a way of greeting the Other, but to greet the Other is already to answer for him. It is difficult to be silent in someone's presence; this difficulty has its ultimate foundation in this signification proper to the saying, whatever is the said. It is necessary to speak of something, of the rain and fine weather, no matter what, but to speak, to respond to him and already answer for him. (*EI* 88)

Saying thus requires a response. Burke suggests, "Prior to and beyond all metaphor, the face is the primary living word, and it demands, it obligates a reply" (Burke 199).

Another significance of saying is that the required response addresses the transcendent. "The incomprehensible nature of the presence of the Other . . . is not to be described negatively. Better than comprehension, *discourse* relates with what remains essentially transcendent" (*TI* 195). In turn, this means that the "[f]ace and discourse are tied" (*EI* 87). Furthermore, "it is discourse, and, more exactly, response or responsibility which is this authentic relationship" (*EI* 88). Language crosses what Sartre calls "the reef of solipsism," not in the said, but in the saying. This might strike us as surprising since thought would seem to be a necessary condition for speech;

but, for Levinas, speech is a necessary condition for thought. Burke notes that "[t]hought is not fundamentally constitutive of meaning, but is astonished to find itself *already operative as speech*, already as word addressed to the Other . . . " (Burke 200).

Levinas characterizes this moment of contact between the self and the transcendent other as proximity. The saying " . . . is the proximity of one to the other . . . " (*OBBE* 5). Proximity is opposed to possession; I cannot be proximate to myself. It is, therefore, to be situated as a neighbor to the other, to be next to . . . The face indicates this immediacy with the other person, this proximity. Since it is beyond the totality of thought, the presence of the other person must be felt as contact, as a force that affects me:

> . . . the proximity of the Other is presented as the fact that the Other is not simply close to me in space, or close like a parent, but he approaches me essentially insofar as I feel myself—insofar as I am--responsible for him. It is a structure that in nowise resembles the intentional relation which in knowledge attaches us to the object—to no matter what object, be it a human object. Proximity does not revert to this intentionality; in particular it does not revert to the fact that the Other is known to me. (*EI* 96-97)

Prior to the distinction between subjects and objects, proximity is contact with an other person. Furthermore, "[t]he passivity undergone in proximity by the force of an alterity in me is the passivity of a recurrence to oneself which is not the alienation of an identity betrayed" (*OBBE* 114). Even though the other person is proximate, I am not crushed by his weight; the other is lord and master, but also widow and orphan. I do not loose my identity in confrontation with alterity. I gain it. Proximity is "the nearness of my neighbor, the corporeal approach and contact of the Other prior to my experience of the Other as other, or myself as self" (Burke 203).

Since proximity is manifested in discourse which crosses the gulf between persons, Levinas claims that proximity is tied to responsibility. "It is a response without question, the immediacy of peace that is incumbent on me" (*OBBE* 139). The other who speaks to me not only demands a response, she also enables it, thereby endowing me with an ability to respond, for Levinas, my respons-*ability*. Before I can respond, I must be addressed. Thus, I cannot be the source of my own responsibility, and this means, in turn, that my responsibility already indicates that the other is not me. As author of my responsibility, the other cannot be possessed—reduced to the self—without also dissolving my responsibility. To kill the other is, then, to destroy the very origin of my responsibility.

Since the epiphany of the other is a correlate of my responsibility, the other calls me into question and makes me answer for myself:

> The fact that the face maintains a relation with me by discourse does not range him in the same; he remains absolute within the relation. The solipsist dialectic of consciousness always suspicious of being in captivity in the same breaks off. For the ethical relationship which subtends discourse is not a species of consciousness whose ray emanates from the I; it puts the I in question. This putting in question emanates from the other. (*TI* 195)

That I am called into question indicates the radical otherness of the other which, again, reveals that the other person comes from beyond my world. She is endowed with an "other worldly" character. In turn, Levinas describes the other as coming from "on high." This revelation, as we shall see, ascribes an identity to the self; I am the one who is not the other precisely because I am responsible to the other.

Before the infinity of the face, the self, taken in a social and interpersonal sense, is born. "Subjectivity is being a hostage" (*OBBE* 127). It arises in confrontation with a dominant other who is never reducible to the same. "The self is a *sub-jectum*; it is under the weight of the universe, responsible for everything. The unity of the universe is not what my gaze embraces in its unity of apperception, but what is incumbent on me from all sides, regards me in the two senses of the term, accuses me, is my affair" (*OBBE* 116). I become a subject by being a subject before an other, by being exposed, and by responding to his command. "The exposure to the other is not something added to the one to bring it from the inward to the outside. Exposedness is the one-in-responsibility, and thus the one in its uniqueness stripped of all protection that would multiply it" (*OBBE* 56). The self, feeling the exterior pass through its world, is already obligated to respond to the transcendent when it passes. In turn, this means that "[t]he latent birth of the subject occurs in an obligation where no commitment was made" (*OBBE* 140). Thus, ethical obligation precedes the birth of a subject, or rather is what gives rise to the subject. This is what Levinas means when he says that subjectivity is the self held hostage by the other. He writes:

> It is through the condition of being hostage that there can be in the world pity, compassion, pardon and proximity—even the little there is, even the simple "After you, sir." The unconditionality of being hostage is not the limit case of solidarity, but the condition for all solidarity. Every accusation and persecution, as all interpersonal praise, recompense, and punishment presuppose the subjectivity of the ego, substitution, the possibility of putting oneself in the place of the other, which refers to the transference from the "by the other" into a "for the other," and in persecution from the outrage inflicted by the other to the expiation for his fault by me. (*OBBE* 117-118)

Here, vulnerability and astonishment are converted into responsibility. To be held hostage is to be held accountable, to be made to "stand for" the other, to be pushed back into my being by the one who faces me.

For Levinas, this situation is essentially one-sided. The transcendent other defines my subjectivity; I may or may not define his. This is because on the level of sensibility, everything unfolds from my perspective. In sensibility, the space between subjects is asymmetrical: "Multiplicity in being, which refuses totalization but takes form as fraternity and discourse, is situated in a 'space' essentially asymmetrical" (*TI* 216). This asymmetrical character of intersubjective space arises from the radical alterity of the other person. Lingis suggests, "The other is not only other than me, but other than the sphere of what is presented to me, other than what can be posited as a being or than what strives to appear. And from this transcendence puts the totality under accusation" (*OBBE* xxxii). In other words, I am limited to my interiority, but the other person arises from the exterior. I am contained, while the other person is not.[12] He enters from the outside, from beyond my world. This, in turn, suggests that he is unforeseeable. I do not know what his next action will be. In a sense, then, the other is protected, given the advantage over the self, because the other may know his next move, while I do not.

The other, therefore, has something that I do not have. Lingis notes that "[t]he other is not experienced as an empty pure place and means for the world to exhibit another perspective, but as a contestation of my appropriation of the world, as a disturbance in the play of the world, a break in its cohesion" (*OBBE* xxiii). The other interrupts my world without being assimilated into it, thereby indicating that the other is beyond the world.

> Man as Other comes to us from the outside, a separated—or holy—face. His exteriority, that is, his appeal to me, is his truth. My response is not added as an accident to a 'nucleus' of his objectivity, but first *produces* his truth (which his 'point of view' upon me can not nullify). (*TI* 291)

The truth of the other person is produced in my response; the meaning of the otherness of the other person is given on this level as that which obligates my response. This is to say that the meaning of otherness is "understood" by me in my obligation and response, not in any conceptual knowledge. Furthermore, this meaning is not found in the content of my response, but in the very act of responding. So, the meaning of the otherness of the other person is already ethical before it is anything else; ethics precedes any theoretical science.

I have already mentioned that Levinas does not envision the other person as intruding on the subject thereby crushing the self; the relationship between the self and other is not one of violence: " . . . the relation [with the other] is maintained without violence, in peace with this absolute alterity. The 'resistance' of the other does not do violence to me, does not act negatively; it has a positive structure: ethical" (*TI* 197). It is true that the other person upsets my world, or disturbs the domain of the same, but the epiphany of the other person is only a disturbance, not death.[13] Hence, Levinas says that the relationship with the other is not violent, but ethical, or not violent precisely because it is ethical. This non-violent condition of the face-to-face encounter is related to the two postures in which the other appears.

The other commands insofar as he comes from on high, but calls insofar as he is destitute and needs my care. Thus, Levinas goes on to suggest:

> The being that presents himself in the face comes from a dimension of height, a dimension of transcendence whereby he can present himself as a stranger without opposing me as obstacle or enemy. More, for my position as *I* consists in being able to respond to this essential destitution of the Other, finding resources for myself. The Other who dominates me in his transcendence is thus the stranger, the widow, and the orphan, to whom I am obligated. (*TI* 215)

While it is difficult to see exactly how Levinas arrives at the destitution of the other from her transcendence, the suggestion seems to be that inasmuch as the other is unforeseeable, she is not essentially any thing (i.e., an object) be it enemy or obstacle. The other is, in fact, (would have to be) a stranger in my world. She is a foreigner in my land, "out of place." Furthermore, the other person is essentially without familial ties in my world; the widow and the orphan are both alone, and vulnerable because they are alone. They are without support in both an ontological and intimate sense. While the other person commands from on high, the very proximity required to make the command also discloses a vulnerable other. The other person, thus, assumes two postures in the epiphany of the face, both of which are essential to ethical responsibility. The dominant posture presents the ethical command; the destitute posture allows the self to put itself in the place of the other, to "substitute" for her, though even this is not an act of the self as much as a passive response.

Levinas notes that substitution *is* the ipseity of the self, suggesting that ethical subjectivity unfolds in taking the place of the other. In substitution, my identity becomes concrete. "In substitution my being that belongs to me and not to another is undone, and it is through this substitution that I am not 'another,' but me" (*OBBE* 127). If Levinas is correct here, the meaning of being a subject is to be for the other, or rather, to be in the place of the other. Substitution cannot be merely the idea of being in the place of the other, for ideas have yet to appear on the scene. Lingis suggests:

> The being singularized and constrained to one's own self converts into a putting oneself in the place of all—and is the same movement, the movement of recurrence which ipseity is. These are not even the passive and active phases of a movement. For one does not bear the burden of others as a result of one's own initiative. One is held to bear the burden of others;

the substitution is a passive effect, which one does not succeed in convert-
ing into an active initiative or into one's own virtue. (*OBBE* xxxi)

Levinas seems to suggest that in being persecuted by another person, I am
made to consider the other person as other. However, since consideration
cannot be granted on the conceptual level, it becomes manifest as a comportment of the self to the other person. I am made to be considerate of the
other—to consider the other *as other*—by the other and for the other's sake.
In substitution one takes on the characteristic of being a mother to all—one
who has been invested with the care of alterity. Burke explains:

> The gestation of the other within me is a forming of me as mother; I real-
> ize the depth of my being for and of the Other, so much so that I *substi-*
> *tute* for the Other: I feel responsible for the suffering he endures from
> others and from life and the suffering he imposes. I am obligated being in
> the heart of my being. (Burke 203)

Substitution is the conversion of my being as a subjection by the other to a
subjection for the other. "I become substantial and a subject, subjected to the
world and to the others. And because in this putting myself in the place of
another I am imperiously summoned, singled out, through it I accede to
singularity" (*OBBE* xxiii). There is no loss of self, but an emergence of self
as an emanation towards the other, though none of this is the result of an
action on the part of the self. Levinas suggests:

> In principle the I does not pull itself out of its "first person"; it supports
> the world. Constituting itself in the very movement wherein being respon-
> sible for the other devolves on it, subjectivity goes to the point of substitu-
> tion for the Other. It assumes the condition—or the uncondition—of hos-
> tage. Subjectivity as such is initially hostage; it answers to the point of
> expiating for others. (*EI* 99-100)

The self, inasmuch as it is a subjection to the other person before the rational
powers of world constitution are set to work, becomes the *moral* support for
the world that it will constitute. Since the transcendent cannot be included
in this world without losing its transcendence, moral support is a matter of
"making room for" the other in my world. Since I must make room for the

other, and since I cannot do this in knowledge without killing the other, making room must be on another level. Substitution, as a result of being held hostage, means supporting the other, who finds no other support besides me in my world. In substitution, I welcome the other into my home.

For Levinas, responsibility arises from the other person in the discourse of the face as my substitution for the other. Thus, his notion of responsibility is much aligned with responsiveness. To be responsive to the other is to respond to the person who addresses me. But this is only one aspect of responsibility; it is clear that, for Levinas, responsibility is more than simple responsiveness. It is, more importantly, the foundation of interpersonal relationships. Sociality unfolds within ethics. Levinas writes:

> The conjuncture in which a man is responsible for other men, the ethical relationship, which is habitually considered as belonging to a derivative or founded order, has been . . . approached as irreducible. It is structured as the-one-for-the-other. It signifies outside of all finality and every system, where finality is but one of the principles of systematization possible. This responsibility appears as a plot without a beginning, anarchic. (*OBBE* 135)

Levinas' notion of responsibility presupposes that prior to the birth of the subject, I am first other-directed, or that perhaps my subjectivity is this other-directedness. It also entails that all thought enters on the scene after the epiphany of the ethical other in the face. So, the other person precedes my ethical subjectivity, and ethics precedes any conceptual endeavor. Inasmuch as responsibility is foundational for interpersonal relations, it is in responsibility that the presence of the other person is tied to my ethical subjectivity. Levinas writes, "In [*Otherwise than Being*] I speak of responsibility as the essential, primary and fundamental structure of subjectivity. For I describe subjectivity in ethical terms" (*EI* 95). Furthermore, "the tie with the Other is knotted only as responsibility" (*EI* 97) as well. Thus, it would appear that responsibility relates the subject to the other, or, in more general terms, ethical obligation binds the subject to the other while maintaining separation. But responsibility is not only what relates one subject to another, it is also the meaning of the otherness of the other *as revealed to the self.* The other person is revealed precisely as the one to whom I am responsible.

Insofar as I am held hostage for the other person, I am made to stand in his place. Thus, I am responsible "for what is not my deed, or for what does not even matter to me; or which precisely does not matter to me, is met by me as face" (*EI* 95). I find myself responsible, dis-inter-ested, divested of my self concerns and made to carry the burden of the other. Levinas writes:

> To be human means to live as if one were not a being among beings. As if, through human spirituality, the categories of being inverted into an "otherwise than being." Not only into a "being otherwise"; being otherwise is still being. The "otherwise than being," in truth, has no verb which would designate the event of its un-rest, its dis-inter-*estedness*, its putting-into-question of this being—or this *estedness*—of the being. (*EI* 100)

The advent of the other person overturns the world order to the point of making the other my concern. In responsibility, "[t]he ontological condition [the rational structures of my world as a world] undoes itself, or is undone, in the human condition or uncondition" (*EI* 100). To be human is to be responsible.

The separation or difference between the same and the transcendent, then, allows us to pinpoint the essence of ethical subjectivity for Levinas. Just as Kant maintains that everything belonging to self-determination (autonomy, pure practical reason, freedom, a good will, acts done for the sake of duty, etc.) belongs to ethics, so too, does Levinas maintain that what belongs to the relationship with the transcendent belongs to ethics. Contact with a transcendent alterity is ethical contact because the relation between self and other (that does not succeed in merging self and other) is maintained precisely as the obligation not to reduce the other to the self, that is, not to kill the other. In the next chapter, I will cast this moral directive into the language of Kant's categorical imperative; the only way to respond to the other without reducing the other to the self is to treat the other as an end-in-itself.

Inasmuch as subjectivity is born from contact with the other person where the self is passive, ethics is not something I choose (it does not result from anything I do), but something that is demanded of me by the very proximity of the other person. Where Kant finds freedom to be the origin of the moral ought, Levinas finds this origin prior to freedom, in confrontation with the other. He agrees that freedom is bound by the moral ought, but he notes that ethical subjectivity, or moral autonomy in Kantian terms, freedom itself, it made obligated by the other. Confrontation with the other endows my freedom with an ought in the very same act that creates it. Levinas writes, " . . . the absolute accusation, prior to freedom, constitutes freedom which, allied to the Good, situates beyond and outside all essence" (*OBBE* 118). To be a finite creature—to be limited by the totality that is my thought, in confrontation with infinity—gives rise to ethical force. Indeed, ethical force or compulsion arises from the inherent *difference* between the same and the other, between totality and infinity. The social self emerges in this awareness or perhaps from it; thus, my subjectivity, construed in its social sense, is born obligated to the other.

Chapter Four

Returning Levinas to the Order of Reason

We have thus discovered what inscribes human nature with an ought, that is, what makes subjectivity, in its deepest sense, obligated to the other. But we still seem to be a long way away from the self-esteem that Descartes paired so intimately with generosity. This is because Levinas' ethics is inherently one-sided. He considers the self's responsibility to the other at the expense of the other's responsibility to the self. In *Ethics and Infinity*, after Levinas presents the self's total responsibility to the other, Philippe Nemo asks, "But is not the Other also responsible in my regard?" Levinas answers, "Perhaps, but that is *his* affair" (*EI* 98). He goes on to note:

> One of the fundamental themes of *Totality and Infinity* . . . is that the intersubjective relation is a non-symmetrical relation. In this sense, I am responsible for the Other without waiting for reciprocity, were I to die for it. Reciprocity is *his* affair. It is precisely insofar as the relationship between the Other and me is not reciprocal that I am subjection to the Other; and I am "subject" essentially in this sense. (*EI* 98)

Generosity, for Descartes, occurs in a being that is independent of the other as a self capable of acting on itself and, therefore, made worthy of self-esteem. Descartes writes that generous souls

> have complete command over their passions. In particular, they have mastery over their desires, and over jealousy and envy, because everything they think sufficiently valuable to be worth pursuing is such that its acquisition depends solely on themselves; over hatred of other people, because they have esteem for everyone; over fear, because of the self-assurance which confidence in their own virtue gives them; and finally over anger, because they have very little esteem for everything that depends on others, and so they never give their enemies any advantage by acknowledging that they are injured by them. (*PWD* I 385)

Apparently, in Descartes, other-directedness makes a return to the self as a recovery from the fundamental exposure that passion indicates. But here, in

Levinas, the asymmetrical relationship seems to preclude this return to the self that relates generosity and self-esteem.

The problem is compounded since Levinas clings to this asymmetry throughout his works in spite of the fact that this element of his thought has brought him much criticism. Indeed, Valevicius writes, "The ethics of Levinas is an excessive ethics; excessive alterity, excessive passivity, excessive responsibility. Indeed, the problem with Levinas's asymmetrical relation to the Other, my total indebtedness to the Other with no reciprocity, is that the Other is like a God to me."[1] The other person is "like a God to me," but as far as Levinas is concerned, I am not "like a God" to the other.

Following similar lines, Derrida writes "That I am also essentially the other's other, and that I know I am, is the evidence of a strange symmetry whose trace appears nowhere in Levinas's descriptions. Without this evidence, I could not desire (or) respect the other in ethical dissymmetry."[2] And Robert Ehman writes:

> Once we admit that the other transcends us in the manner that Sartre and Levinas describe, there are, after all, only two possible approaches to the other. Either we must struggle to negate his transcendence and thereby save ourselves from domination or else give ourselves over to the other in an endeavor to fulfill his unlimited demands.[3]

Behind these observations is hiding a supposition about what would constitute an ethical imperative for Levinas.

Levinas' notion of responsibility involves an inherent respect for other persons. The other is first, comes before my own self concerns, and is consequently the one to whom I am, first and foremost, responsible. This respect for persons echoes the Kantian ideal of persons as ends-in-themselves, though certainly Levinas will not wish to accept Kant's line of rational argumentation. He writes:

> If one had the right to retain one trait from a philosophical system and neglect all the details of its architecture . . . we would think here of Kantism, which finds a meaning to the human without measuring it by ontology and outside the question 'What is there here . . . ?' that one would like to take to be preliminary . . . (OBBE 129)

The fact that Kant finds this worth in our rational nature does not appear to bother Levinas. Kant recognizes the radical autonomy of the other person as one who cannot be used strictly for my advantage. This notion is consonant with Levinas: the other person is autonomous, cannot be reduced to the totality, and therefore is the one who issues the command, "thou shalt not kill." The roots of Levinas' ethical metaphysics are planted deeply within the autonomy of the other.

In moments, Levinas comes close to suggesting that normative morality is grounded in something analogous to Kant's third formulation of the categorical imperative: "Act in such a way that you treat humanity, whether in your own person or in the person of another, always at the same time as an end and never simply as a means."[4] But Levinas only comes close. He does not present a categorical imperative, and it is clear that he would not accept this formulation. It hangs on Kant's postulate that "rational nature exists as an end-in-itself" (*GMM* 36). Since all humans have a rational nature, and the moral subject is human, Kant is able to add the qualifier "whether in your own person or in the person of another" to his imperative. Levinas, on the other hand, does not find the source of moral obligation in something that is inherent in each human being as part of his nature, but in the transcendence of the other person. This means, in turn, that only before an other person am I commanded to responsibility. If I am not the other's other, then there is nothing in me, or in the other's relation to me, that will command responsibility for me to the other person or myself. I have no grounds on which to claim rights for myself in the face of the other. Hence, it would appear that a normative ethics in the style of Levinas would be more other-directed than it is in Kant. Perhaps, then, we might suggest that Levinas' imperative would look like this: "Treat the other person as an end-in-itself," or, in keeping true to existential vocabulary, "Comport yourself towards the other person in such a way that your being is always for-the-other." Indeed, this formula suggests Levinas' description of ethical subjectivity as the self held hostage by the other person, made to stand in the place of the other, responsible to and for the other, for what is not even my deed. But application of this imperative to normative situations would reveal problems in

Levinas' thought. If all ethics arises from the other person, and the self is not considered as an "other person," then ethics does not apply to the self. I can have no complaint against the other for not treating me ethically. The self seems to have all the responsibilities and no rights, since the very demand that the other person be ethical in my regard is a category mistake, an attempt to apply the category of responsibility outside of the domain in which responsibility is defined.

Without some notion of self-responsibility and responsibility for me on the part of the other, the command of the other would seem to demand that I hand over all my possessions to the other. Would I not then be left impoverished, comporting my entire being towards the other? Robert Walsh writes, "[For Levinas], our very freedom is already in the grip of the for-the-other. Political society is an emanation of responsibility. Thus, to act for-myself, for my own gain, my good, my pleasure, is already an aberration of the fundamental situation of responsibility."[5] What then can Levinas offer to normative situations involving killing the other person in self-defense? Such an act would appear to be unjustified, indeed, unjustifiable, on Levinasian grounds. Any situation where the needs and desires of the self are in conflict with the needs and desires of the other appears to be ethically resolvable only by giving myself over to the other and allowing him to have his way. To act otherwise would be, as Walsh suggests, "an aberration of the fundamental situation of responsibility." Enjoyment is egoism, and egoism is unethical before the other.

It would seem that in our search for other persons we have lost the self as a person. Yet, both the self and the other person are necessary for an ethical, intersubjective relationship. Is an ethics that cannot ground self-responsibilities, or responsibilities on the part of the other person for me, a satisfactory ethics? Can such an ethics offer any insight into concrete moral problems where self-concerns are pitted against the concerns of others? Any adequate ethics must account for these other responsibilities, and on this ground, it would appear that Levinas is somehow deficient. So goes this common criticism.

We must remember, however, that Levinas never actually presents an ethics. In fact, he writes, "One can without doubt construct an ethics in function of what I have . . . said, but this is not my own theme" (*EI* 90). So, any attempt to address normative considerations without first attempting to construct a Levinasian ethics is premature. In this sense, the criticisms presented above cannot be addressed against Levinas' ethics; properly speaking, he does not have one. His project located the origin of moral responsibility; he determined how freedom becomes endowed with its ought. He did not determine what this means for normative considerations, and admittedly, it is difficult at the outset to see precisely how one might get from Levinas' metaphysical grounding of moral responsibility to an ethics. Certainly, this gesture must involve a movement from the originary situation of responsibility to an ethics in which I can make use of the fact that I am the other's other.

Levinas indicates that he has not yet taken his originary ethical metaphysics to this point. Contrary to Derrida's claim noted above, "[t]hat I am also essentially the other's other, and that I know I am, is the evidence of a strange symmetry whose trace appears nowhere in Levinas' descriptions," Levinas writes, " . . . if the other can invest me and invest my freedom, of itself arbitrary, this is in the last analysis because I myself can feel myself to be the other of the other. But this comes about only across very complex structures" (*TI* 84). He does not analyze these structures; he simply notes that they are.

Before we can assess a normative point of view that follows from Levinas, it is vital that we consider what some of these "complex structures" might be. To do so, we must continue Levinas' account beyond his descriptions while remaining true to them. We must begin to complete Levinas' account of the self in relation to the other person in order to establish ethical reciprocity. Once the self is viewed as the other's other—that is, as an other person who issues a moral command to the other person—the possibility of mutual relationship opens up, and with it, the possibility of ethical norms to balance the needs and desires of the self against those of the other. How we might provide a moral grounding for the self as the other's other thereby entering into a common moral terrain with the other is the topic of this chapter.

The Other's Command and My Freedom

Levinas legitimates self-concerns by the entry of the third party into the social relation. Lingis writes, " . . . the entry of a third party, treating me as an other alongside of the other I faced, first institutes a kind of common terrain among us. I am, thanks to him, someone to be concerned about, someone to answer for" (*OBBE* xxxv). Though the entry of the third party provides interesting material for phenomenological analysis, it does not get us out of our difficulty. The ethical imperative still arises in the face-to-face relationship. A glance cast from the side-lines, though it might set up a common terrain, does not exhibit the character of subjecting both of us in what was once the face-to-face relationship to the third person. The third person does not reverse the originary asymmetry of the interpersonal relation, rather he institutes a new order. Hence, the third person is not of immediate concern to us here. What is needed is a means of recognizing that I am the other's other in the context of the face-to-face relationship. This recognition must involve tipping the scales of asymmetry.

Sartre's analysis of "the look" indicates how we might begin to understand this reversal. In "the look" I do not just see the face of the other person, I feel my being-for-the-other.[6] The look reveals my being-for-the-other precisely because the other looks *at me*. In *Being and Nothingness*, Sartre analyzes the look from the viewpoint of shame. But he also notes that my being-for-the-other can be revealed in pride. Though he does not analyze the look from this perspective, doing so would reveal that before the other person I am made worth-while. I am not always guilty before the other. I am not only subjected to the other in the look; the other also confirms my existence. We can see this point in a telling passage from Sartre's biography of Baudelaire:

> The child takes his parents for gods. Their actions like their judgments are absolute. They are the incarnation of universal Reason, law, and the mean-ing and purpose of the world. When the eye of these divine beings is

turned on him [Baudelaire], their look is enough to justify him at once to the very roots of his existence. It confers on him a definite, sacred character. Since they are infallible, it follows that they *see* him as he really *is*. There is no room in his mind for hesitation or doubt. True, all that he sees of himself is the vague succession of his moods, but the gods have made themselves the guardians of his eternal essence. He knows that it exists; even though he can have no direct experience of it, he realizes that his *truth* does not consist in what he can know of himself, but that it is hidden in the large, terrible yet gentle eyes which are turned towards him. He is a real essence among other real essences; he has *his* place in the world—an absolute place in an absolute world.[7]

To be before a "god," or one who is deified in an interpersonal relationship, is not only to fall prey to the demands of this "god"; it also involves discovering a part of myself in the context of this relation.

My subjectivity, originating as a subjection to the other person, is nonetheless mine, though this aspect of my self is dependent on the other, and as such, it places me at his hands. For Sartre, the self attempts to guarantee this dependence by engaging in various relationships (e.g., love, hate, sadism, masochism, etc.), but each attempt is ultimately doomed to failure. The freedom of the other always keeps the self in question. On this point, Levinas and Sartre agree, though Levinas sees it as the possibility of peace where Sartre sees it as a motive to deny the transcendence of the other (*BN* 473-474). But Sartre also indicates that before another person who is like a god, the self becomes like a god. Here, we find good reason not to deny the transcendence of the other. "Since the Other is the foundation of my being, he could not be dissolved in me without my being-for-others disappearing" (*BN* 476). Thus the self is dependent on the other for an intimate part of its selfhood, its social self. Since it is also independent of the other—after all, it can deny the other who is passing judgment on it—the self wants to deny the transcendence of the other and secure its independence without denying itself. It wants to be God. Since it cannot both deny and not deny the transcendence of the other at the same time, interpersonal relationships, for Sartre, are always marked with conflict.

In what follows, I treat the interpersonal relationship as the existential possibility of law (i.e., normative ethics) situated upon Levinas' ethical metaphysics. Somewhere between Sartre's analysis of the look and Levinas' analysis of the face-to-face a more complete description of the face-to-face situation unfolds. Taking both Sartre and Levinas seriously, the structure of interpersonal relationship does not mean that the other person alone is dominant, even though he is ethically prior. This becomes clear when we realize that the being who tends to say "no" to the other in Sartre is the very being who ought to say "yes" in Levinas. Though the ethical command may arise initially from a dominant other, my possibility of saying "yes" or "no" to the other person compromises his dominance. In turn, the other is subjected to my moral freedom. The other becomes destitute, not in the earlier sense of being without support in the world, but in the more immediate sense of being vulnerable before my freedom. I am free (i.e., able) to kill the other, but obligated not to do so.

My freedom to say "yes" or "no" to the other's command, indicates that I am unforeseeable to the other. The command of the other person is expressed as authority, not necessity. As such, it may or may not be obeyed. But this means that the other cannot know what my response will be—whether or not I will obey his command—and, thus, that I cannot be totalized by the other. If I cannot be inscribed within the totality that defines the other's world, then I must transcend it. That I know this prior to my actual response and *that I may play it to my advantage*—even though I ought not—is already an indication that I am the other's other. This means, in turn, that the other can be my moral authority only insofar as she is vulnerable before my freedom. The very command of the other already places her at my hands.

This characterization of the other person as one who is subjected to my freedom is revealed in a closer analysis of the ethical command, "thou shalt not kill." Indeed, this very command reveals the other's vulnerability, as Levinas notes. When the other speaks this command, he also confesses that he is precisely the type of being that can be killed and that the self (his other) is capable of this murderous act. Furthermore, since the other does not know whether I will obey his command and knows that I am free not to, the command must also be a plea, not merely the distant "thou shalt not kill," but the more immediate and pressing, "please do not kill." The ethical command begs in the same gesture that it commands.

These themes are illustrated in the context of the Clutter Murders, which Truman Capote documented in his book, *In Cold Blood*.[8] On November 15, 1959, Richard Hickock and Perry Smith broke into a small Kansas farmhouse and systematically murdered Mr. and Mrs. Clutter, their daughter, Nancy, and their son. The only apparent motive for the crime was Hickock's need to assert his dominance over others. He writes, "When I got into that house I was going to show them who was boss."[9] For the sake of analysis, I wish to take a closer look at the murders from Hickock's perspective, treating him as the self in Levinas' framework.

In order to situate Hickock into the role of the Levinas' self, it is important to note, first of all, that he was susceptible to the ethical command issuing from the face of the other. Before committing the murders, Hickock plans to rape Nancy. But in meeting her face-to-face, Hickock remembers, " . . . I lost all desire to do anything to her at all. I don't know why. I could feel the blood rush to my head when she looked at me. It seemed she was reading my mind. All of a sudden I was ashamed of what I was thinking" (Hickock 15). Hickock lies to her telling her that he "had never hurt anyone before and that [he] wasn't going to start then" (Hickock 15). He felt himself "getting pretty soft-hearted" (Hickock 15). After all, he had come to the house to assert his dominance over others. Now he was having second thoughts. Somewhere between his desire for dominance and his obligation in the face-to-face encounter with the young girl, Hickock catches himself:

> I wondered to myself if I was [going to hurt someone]. I had just given up the idea of trying to be tough. I remember that I thought I ought to be real proud of myself, wanting to be tough and impress some one [sic] when all I had to be tough with was an elderly woman and a young kid. A feeling of reproach came over me. Then I thought to myself, why lie about it? Am I the one who is boss or not? (Hickock 15)

Hickock mentions that, at this moment, he could have been talked into leaving the house without committing murder. He was caught by the command, "thou shalt not kill," and then given the opportunity to respond. How he was going to respond was unforeseeable to everyone involved.

For whatever reasons, Hickock committed the crimes with Smith. After joining Smith in the basement to shoot the father and son, Hickock and Smith return to shoot Nancy. This shooting is particularly interesting in that Nancy was the only member of the family who was not gagged; she could speak. Having heard the two previous shots, she must have known of the murderers' intents when they entered her room. With her murder close at hand, Nancy does not say "thou shalt not kill," rather she pleads, "Oh, no! Oh, please! No! No! No! No! Don't! Oh, please don't! Please!" (Capote 276). This telling expression speaks the distant ethical command issuing from a transcendent face, to be sure, but in light of the close proximity of murder. Thus, it is spoken in vulnerability. Here, Levinas' asymmetry has shifted its polarity. Nancy knows that she can be killed, and having heard the previous shots, she is well aware that Smith and Hickock are able to kill her. Her command is a plea. Yet, she cannot know whether her plea will be heard. In this case it was not.

Looking back on the entire incident, Hickock expresses the profound sense of control and dominance he experienced: "As I think about it now I realize it was fun. Nobody was telling us what to do. We were boss in that house. It felt good to be able to do as I damn well pleased. No orders, no bosses, no nothing" (Hickock 18). Dominance was achieved by killing the dominant other; it consisted of overcoming the moral authority of the face, of denying God. He writes:

> When the Judge was telling the jury what a good job they had done I thought that these pompous old ginks were the lousiest looking specimens of manhood I had ever seen; old cronies that acted like they were God or somebody.
>
> Right then I wished every one of them had been at the Clutter house that night and that included the Judge. I would have found out how much God they had in them! If they had been there and had any God in them I would have let it run out on the floor. (Hickock 24)

Until the very end, Hickock clings to the need to be justified by the look of others. "When the jury filed out of the courtroom not one of them would look at me. I looked at each one in the face and I kept thinking, Look at me, look at me, look at me! But none of them would" (Hickock 24).

The very possibility of denying the other person indicates to the other that I am free in spite of whatever he may command or think, even if my freedom is made possible by his command. This makes me unforeseeable to the other, and as such, I transcend the other's world. As transcendent to the other—revealed precisely in the possibilities confronting me in my freedom—I know that I cannot be totalized by the other. A mutual unforeseeableness between one other to his other is reflected in commanding and the concomitant possibility of saying "no" that this command opens up. Though the other issues his command in the first moment of interpersonal contact, this command at the same time opens up my moral freedom, which means that I can violate the other, even though I ought not. In turn, this reverses Levinas' asymmetry; the other is exposed before my freedom, placing him at my hands. This exposure—a metaphysical consequent of the other's command—in turn raises the self to a position of dominance over the other. Thus, the interpersonal relationship, though at first asymmetrical with a dominant other, reverses its asymmetry in my very freedom that the other in his dominance gives me. The face-to-face relationship, while not properly speaking symmetrical, is mutually asymmetrical, and in the vibrations of this asymmetry moral authority is overthrown by the possibility of moral agreement. What is, at first, a tyrannical moral order with an authoritarian other becomes the metaphysical possibility of a "social" contract. The command "thou shalt not kill" converts to a mutual "let us not kill one another" the moment the other commands me, thereby sacrificing himself to my possibility. We have thus discovered the metaphysical meaning behind "response" taken in its etymological sense as "to promise in return." In the dynamics between the other's command and my promise in return, this covenant relation becomes the metaphysical possibility of law and social order.

Concrete Experience and Moral Freedom

Without contesting Levinas' asymmetry, we have found that the complex structures involved in knowing that I am the other's other include an awareness of my own freedom. But, at the same time, this awareness is precisely the realization that I am able to take one of two courses; I may obey the moral imperative of the other or I may deny it. Whatever the outcome of my action may be, it is my deed. I am responsible for it. As such, my choice reflects back on me. I am guilty when I fail to live up to the moral imperative imposed on me by the transcendence of the other. I am not guilty when I choose the proper path and make my actions moral. So, even though the other wages the ethical command, my response, whether good or bad, reflects on me. As Descartes notes, "the exercise of our free will and the control we have over our volitions" provides the only "good reason for esteeming ourselves" (*PWD* I 384).

Hiding in the backround here is a conception of freedom as moral, a choice between right and wrong, and not freedom as preferential, a choice between desires.[10] Levinas recognizes both modes of autonomy in his Talmudic commentary, "And God Created Women." He writes:

> The drama of existence is not only that existence is divided into choices between desires but that existence is also suspended between the Law that is given me and my nature, which is incapable of submitting to the Law without constraint. It is not freedom which defines the human being. It is obedience which defines him.[11]

Here, Levinas notes that the law must come from beyond desire. Earlier I noted that it is revealed precisely as the contestation of desire, as a resistance to my egoistic tendency to possess. If moral freedom is a necessary condition for true self-esteem, and if this freedom is given to me as a contestation of my desire, then the existential condition for my self-esteem resides in the face-to-face situation. The other who looks at me gives me my freedom, without which I could not be responsible for my actions and without which I could not be praised or blamed for my deed. The command of the other is,

thus, the existential condition of my self-esteem. I will attempt to make this explicit in what follows, though much remains to be clarified beforehand; for instance, it is necessary to clarify the extent to which my *moral* freedom depends on the other. To do this, I will borrow from Kant's *Grounding for the Metaphysics of Morals*.

Kant, like Levinas, sees the moral situation primarily in terms of a contest between desire and obligation. Indeed, following Levinas we have entered that domain of inquiry that Kant calls the "metaphysics of morals," though we have entered it from an existential as opposed to an ideal perspective. Kant's good will is good precisely because of its commitment and obedience to the moral law. For Kant, as for Descartes, self-respect or esteem is attainable only by participation in the "drama of existence," only by becoming a moral agent, that is, by acknowledging the moral law within and responding accordingly. But, as I have said, we have entered into the "metaphysics of morals" from an existential perspective rather than from Kant's ideal perspective. Before turning to the ideal sphere—which we will do shortly—it will be helpful for us to examine the moral situation existentially on the level of Levinas' ethical metaphysics, but in light of Kant's observations concerning the nature of moral experience.

Early on in *The Grounding*, Kant begins an analysis of the concept of the good will to determine which other concepts might be aligned with it. To this end, he analyzes human acts. These are acts that proceeds from the will, and that, therefore, require a motive. There are two possible motives for human acts: they may follow from the desires of the body (inclination) or the dictates of duty (here, the moral law). This immediately leads to three classifications of acts. Some acts violate duty, but follow an inclination. Since these acts disagree with the moral law, Kant notes right off that they cannot proceed from a good will.

In the second place, some acts follow an inclination, but still accord with duty. Kant further divides these acts into two sub-categories, noting that there are two kinds of inclinations, mediate and immediate. Acts that follow a mediate inclination, but still accord with duty, are done with an ulterior motive in mind, like helping my boss change a flat tire because I know that he is writing performance appraisals next week and I want a raise. Here, the motive of my act is getting a raise, not changing a tire or helping a person in need. Kant notes that these acts are immoral because they are not done with duty in mind, but with the hopes of satisfying a desire.

Acts that follow an immediate inclination, but still accord with duty, are acts that are done because I am naturally inclined to do them. Here, I will use Kant's example: "To be beneficent where one can is a duty; and besides this, there are many persons who are so sympathetically constituted that, without any further motive of vanity or self-interest [that is, without a mediate inclination], they find an inner pleasure in spreading joy around them and can rejoice in the satisfaction of others as their own work" (*GMM* 11). These people are in the fortunate situation of having inclinations that truly accord with the moral law. To the surprise of most first time readers of Kant's ethics, however, Kant remarks that such actions have "no true moral worth" (*GMM* 11). These acts are not immoral, but amoral.

Morality is restricted to the third type of human acts. These acts accord with the moral law, but they violate desire. Therefore, they must be done for the sake of the moral law. Kant presents the following example for acts in this category:

> Suppose then the mind of [a] friend of mankind to be clouded over with his own sorrow so that all sympathy with the lot of others is extinguished, and suppose him still to have the power to benefit others in distress, even though he is not touched by their trouble because he is sufficiently absorbed with his own; and now suppose that, even though no inclination moves him any longer, he nevertheless tears himself from this deadly insensibility and performs the action without any inclination at all, but solely from duty—then for the first time his action has genuine moral worth. (*GMM* 11)

Again, first time reader's of Kant are often struck by what, admittedly, looks like a counter-intuitive situation. The person who does his duty and wants to do so appears to be less moral than the person who does his duty but does not want to do so. After all, the former is amoral, while the latter is moral. This very observation, however, reflects a belief that the person with a morality is always better than the person without one. But this is not the case when we realize that the person whose inclinations accord with duty is preferable to the person who does his duty in divergence from his inclination precisely because the former, the amoral agent in this picture, *has no need of morality at all*. When we keep this in mind, it is easy to see why Kant exempts agents with immediate inclinations that accord with duty from his analysis of morality. Since they are not involved in a *moral* contest, they are irrelevant to his analysis.

If we follow Husserl and Levinas for a moment and steer clear of naturalism—that is, the tendency to reify objects on the basis of appearances in experience and then use these objects to explain the very appearances from which they were derived—we can get an existential perspective on Kant's hierarchy of human acts. To do this, we must avoid the temptation to reify morality itself. We must drop the intellectual pretension that morality *is* something that exists always in some ideal world, that it somehow comes apart from the moral situation in which it is disclosed, and take a closer look at what is going on in Kant's analysis of concepts presented above. Kant, like Levinas, has characterized the moral situation precisely as a divergence between inclination and the moral law, between what I want to do and what I ought to do. Only when the two diverge is there a choice between right and wrong. Thus, beings who are not caught in this divergence are not moral agents—they have no *choice* between right and wrong—and, consequently, they are not morally free. Only when this divergence opens up does freedom become actual. Only when desire is contested can moral autonomy emerge as a fact of human existence. Thus, if we are seeking the existential condition under which morality first makes its appearance, we must look for the condition of divergence, not between desires, but between a desire and the contestation of desire.[12] For Levinas, this condition is the face-to-face situation that resists my desire to possess. More profoundly, since desire precisely is, in essence, always a desire for possession, the face-to-face situation is disclosed as a resistance to desire itself.

Levinas has pointed us in the right direction for finding the existential grounding for morality by examining the condition of its appearance in the concrete experience of the human being. Morality and freedom, viewed as moments in concrete experience as opposed to concepts situated within consciousness, become actual only in the encounter with the other. This divergence is revealed as the handing down of the moral law in the concrete situation of the face-to-face. Only later in the recovery from the face-to-face can we reify the moral law—originally a command to perform my action in the present moment, and not a rule or code to govern my behavior—as "morality" and examine it and all that it entails as a "metaphysics of morals." Levinas' contribution to ethics is that concrete morality must remain prior to any rational construction of ethics, since it is only in the immediate situation of the face-to-face that freedom and the moral law are concretely mine.

To characterize Levinas' ethical metaphysics in relation to Kant, we can say that Levinas analyzes the very moment where I am endowed with the moral ought and set to being morally free. Kant's analysis follows in the wake of this moment, presupposing it in the background. In fact, Kant confesses that he is analyzing what freedom and morality must entail, if they are anything at all. He cannot prove freedom, though he notes that "we must presuppose it if we want to think of a being as rational and as endowed with consciousness of its causality as regards actions, i.e., as endowed with a will" (*GMM* 51). Kant's analysis unfolds within this hypothesis of freedom; Levinas' unfolds within the moments when that freedom is made concrete. In finding the originary point of divergence that manifests concrete morality in human experience, Levinas fills in a missing piece to Kant's moral puzzle. In so doing, he provides an existential grounding to Kant's idealist ethics.

Moral Experience and the Law

So far, we have isolated the existential conditions necessary for moral autonomy and responsibility. We have found these in the divergence between an egoist desire and the moral ought, which is nothing other than the contestation of desire by a moral authority. Since this ought is not a desire, it must come from beyond the egoism that defines the human being. Levinas locates it in the transcendent face of the other. Furthermore, since the very conditions that define moral autonomy do so by opening up the concrete possibility of moral freedom, moral responsibility is not defined by a pre-existing freedom; it is, instead, the very condition of this freedom.

Having isolated the conditions of moral autonomy, however, we have still to make the transition from Levinas to a normative ethics. We now understand the existential structure of the ought; it is the directive not to possess the other. But we have yet to determine the content of the law that this directive imposes on experience. To help in this task, I will appeal to Kant's approach to ethics and, in particular, to the categorical imperative.

At first, using Kant in this capacity might seem to present problems. Kant derives the moral law from freedom while Levinas sees inscription within the law as the very condition of freedom. So, Levinas' ethics unfolds prior to freedom while Kant's follows upon it. But when we remember that Levinas is not actually offering an ethics as much as he is presenting the condition for any ethics at all, the situation does not appear problematic. If Kant can derive the moral law from freedom, this is only because freedom is endowed with an ought, a condition necessary to raise moral autonomy from a choice between inclinations to a choice between inclination and duty. To characterize the relationship between Levinas' thought and Kant's ethics, then, it might be helpful to consider the former's project as a fundamental metaphysics of morals that underlies Kant's metaphysics as its very condition, in the same way that Heidegger's fundamental ontology underlies the ontological tradition. This means that Kant's ethics departs from Levinas' existential grounding and, in so doing forms a moral law within the rational order. This extension from existence to the order of essences transforms Levinas' existential ethics of the concrete into an ethics of universal reason.

However, this transformation involves us in a bit of a difficulty, since in moving from existence to essence, it unties the existential condition that makes rational ethics possible, that is the tie with the other, because in reason there can be no other, as we have established earlier in this work. In Kant, we see this necessary tie with an existential other dissolved in the universalizing character of thought. The other in Kant is not the concrete other that I face, but the idea of the other as a being free and, therefore, worthy of my moral consideration. She is not the author of my moral freedom, because she, too, belongs to the rational order in which Kant's ethics unfolds. In this order, no one is morally distinguishable from anyone else. Thus, in place of Levinas' asymmetry, Kant's rational order institutes a symmetry of such a radical nature that there can be no distinction between self and other in determining the content of the law. Kant notes that after having stripped the will from its inclinations, " . . . there is nothing left to serve the will as [moral] principle except the universal conformity of its actions to law as such, i.e., I should never act except in such a way that I can also will that my maxim should become a universal law" (*GMM* 14). This universal conformity suggests that my actions are moral only if I can perform them without having to make an exception for myself.

This imperative has a rather disturbing result. It means that moral action dissolves the individual into the universal. Being moral is a matter of sacrificing my individuality to the universal conformity of law as such. Worse yet, the moral law neutralizes the very otherness of the other in the universal as well. If Levinas is correct that the moral imperative of the face is "thou shalt not kill," then the very move into universal reason that neutralizes the other and that makes normative ethics possible, is, in the first instance, immoral. Kantian ethics inscribes the other within the horizons of universal reason thereby violating Levinas' existential grounding which strictly prohibits this gesture. This means that, if Kant's ethics correctly articulates morality within the rational order, it must somehow be justified by its existential foundation.

Yet, on the other hand, Kant's ethics correctly articulates Levinas' existential ethics within the horizons of reason, because it precisely states the moral injunction that arises from the face-to-face. Though this might not be apparent when we take Levinas' injunction as "thou shalt not kill," it becomes apparent when we look at what this prohibition against murder really means. It is an injunction not to kill the other by denying his transcendence, by reducing him to the same. Its content thus expresses the realization that the other does not belong to the self; he is not there to be a means to the self's egoistic ends. Rather, he is an end-in-himself. So, the face of the other indicates that I am not to deny the other as end-in-himself. Kant's ethics articulates this situation in the categorical imperative—"Act in such a way that you treat humanity, whether in your own person or in the person of another, always at the same time as an end and never simply as a means" (*GMM* 36). This imperative expresses the content of the law handed down in the face-to-face situation. As such, it is the moral law said within language—hence, within universal reason—that necessarily accompanies the saying by which the command is handed down. Expressing this necessary connection between the saying and the said in general, Levinas writes, "That the *saying* must bear a *said* is the necessity of the same order as that which imposes a society with laws, institutions and social relations" (*EI* 88). Here, we find Levinas' general comment particularized with respect to the moral law. As soon as the imperative of the face is said within language, it becomes the categorical imperative.

Though Kant's imperative violates Levinas' existential grounding precisely by representing in the said the concrete moral situation of the saying, it does so in a very particular way. If we are careful to note the nature of this violation—which is precisely this transition from existence to essence—it is possible to recover a directive from Levinas that might justify Kant's approach. We must find a way to unsay what is said in the categorical imperative, thereby returning it to an original signification that goes beyond the said. This return will provide us with the ultimate sanction of the categorical imperative in the concrete and will, therefore, affirm the value of this imperative within reason. The mechanics of this transformation will be taken up in the next section with the help of Kierkegaard.

For the time being, however, we can observe that the content of the moral law, revealed in the categorical imperative as Levinas' existential imperative signified, will be derived in the manner of Kant. Thus, Levinas' existential ethics transforms into Kant's normative ethics. Furthermore, since the transformation from existence to essence neutralizes the self and other placing them on an equal level within the rational order, the self is due the same moral consideration as the other. The self attains rights through this transformation; but these rights neither supersede nor replace the self's responsibility to the other. Since Kantian ethics are founded on the concrete situation of the face-to-face which gives me my moral freedom in the same gesture that it obligates it, my rights are also founded on the concrete situation. We have, therefore, managed to raise the self to the level of the other where social institutions and the law are concerned and, in so doing, have provided justice for all within the social order. But the very transformation that has permitted us to grant rights to all, including the self, entails that it is only by being responsible in the concrete that one has rights within the social arena.[13]

Kierkegaard and the Inversion of Kantian Ethics

Since the transition from existence to essence predicates moral agency to free beings, and since the self is free—even if this freedom is opened up by the unforeseeability (freedom) of the other, which is always prior—both the self and the other are due moral rights. All of this comes at a cost, for the existential relationship is always asymmetrical. The other is always prior to the self. But if the transition from existence to essence levels out this asymmetry by inscribing the other within the law, we have violated Levinas' injunction not to possess the other. As transcendent, he is always situated beyond the rational order. So, if Kant's ethics are going to remain ethical while signifying Levinas' existential ethics, it must be justified. Fortunately, this transition from the immediacy of the face-to-face to normative ethics has already been thoroughly documented for us by Kierkegaard in *Fear and Trembling*.

This treatise attempts to justify Kantian ethics by examining the priority of faith over ethics where faith places the individual "in an absolute relation to the absolute"[14] and ethics "annul[s] [the individual's] singularity in order to become the universal" (*FT* 54). That the universal order is being justified in this work is admitted in the "Preface"; after seven times denying having anything to do with "the system," Kierkegaard writes, "I invoke everything good for the system . . . " (*FT* 8). The system undoubtedly refers to Hegel's system, as becomes clear later in the work. But insofar as the system is the domain of universal reason, it is moral in the style of Kant. Kierkegaard writes, "The ethical as such is the universal, and as the universal it applies to everyone, which from another angle means that it applies at all times" (*FT* 54).

Kierkegaard, being a strong advocate of individuality, is concerned about ethics construed in this manner. "The single individual, sensately and psychically qualified in immediacy, is the individual who has his *telos* in the universal, and it is his ethical task continually to express himself in this, to annul his singularity in order to become the universal" (*FT* 54). On his reading of Kant and Hegel, being moral is a matter of sacrificing one's individuality to the universal moral order, to the system. But, Kierkegaard writes, "As soon as the single individual asserts himself in his singularity before the universal, he sins . . . " (*FT* 54). Since the command of the other singularizes me, according to Levinas, by demanding that I myself respond as an individual, the very responsibility that is incumbent upon me is already a rupture of the universal order. According to Lingis, "[In substitution] I become substantial and a subject, subjected to the world and to the others. And because in this putting myself in the place of another I am imperiously summoned, singled out, through it I accede to singularity" (*OBBE* xxiii). The very command of the other that singularizes me—thereby making me emerge as the single individual outside of the universal order and supplying the necessary breach of totality needed to make Levinas' ethical foundations ethical—already means that I have sinned. Our problem is not only that Kantian ethics is in need of justification by Levinas' existential foundations, but also, according to Kant and Hegel (following Kierkegaard's reading), that Levinas' existential foundations are in need of justification as well. The two approaches seem incompatible, since by each other's standard, the other is immoral.

Paradoxically, Kierkegaard notes that the system (or the universal order of reason) was designed for the individual, not the individual for the system. If the system is to be justified, it must be returned to the individual for whom and by whom it was designed. But, to continue this paradox, the very return of the universal order to the individual for whom and by whom it was designed, justifies it. The central task of *Fear and Trembling* is to argue that faith is prior to ethics and that ethics is, therefore, justified by its suspension in the "leap of faith."

This paradoxical structure is indicated through the use of several analogies, most notably the relationship between Abraham and Isaac. In being willing to sacrifice his son, Isaac, at God's command, Abraham gets Isaac back, but everything is changed. In a similar manner, the individual, in sacrificing universality as an act of obedience to God, gets the universal back, redeemed. " . . . [T]he movement of faith must continually be made by virtue of the absurd, but yet in such a way, please note, that one does not lose the finite, but gains it whole and intact" (*FT* 37). Keeping in mind that the universal order is the totality discussed by Levinas and is, therefore, finite as opposed to the infinite transcendence of the other that disturbs this order, we can see what Kierkegaard's "leap of faith" means for our purposes. This paradox of faith suggests that "suspending" Kant's universal ethics in the immediacy of the face-to-face where the moral authority originates will ultimately return us to the rational order of Kantian ethics. In turn, this departure from and return to the universal will justify Kant's universal ethics. If Kierkegaard is correct, by giving up Kantian ethics in favor of the individualizing characteristic of the face-to-face situation, we should get Kant back, redeemed.

To understand Kierkegaard's paradox of faith in light of the current project, we must imagine that Levinas' existential ethics unfolds on the level of Kierkegaard's faith. We should do this, however, without going so far as to claim that Levinas and Kierkegaard are undertaking the same project. Levinas is concerned with the origin of the ethical command which makes me responsible to the other. But Kierkegaard is concerned with what happens in response to this command. Thus, Kierkegaard's analysis unfolds after the command of the other has been waged. In addition, his story is told from the perspective of the self who must choose between God's command and his own desire. This it to say that Levinas' analysis precedes Kierkegaard's in that it also provides the existential condition for the leap of faith that Kierkegaard analyzes in *Fear and Trembling*.

The significance of this difference cannot be underestimated. Levinas explicitly denies that he is working from the perspective of Kierkegaard. He writes, "It is not I who resist the system, as Kierkegaard thought; it is the other" (*TI* 40). Thanks to this telling quote from Levinas, we are able to place the "leap of faith" precisely in the context of Levinas' thought, namely, at the moment of response to the infinite other who disrupts the universal order. Levinas' story is told from the moment the infinite other ruptures the universal order (the totality) and demands something of the self. Kierkegaard's story is told from the perspective of faith, which is obedient submission to the command of the infinite other. Kierkegaard writes, "Faith is preceded by a movement of infinity" (*FT* 69) and, later on the same page, " . . . only when the individual has emptied himself in the infinite, only then has the point been reached where faith can break through" (*FT* 69). So, Kierkegaard's story is told from the perspective of the individual already singled out and made free by the command of the other.

Having distinguished the domain of Levinas' work from that of Kierkegaard's, we can now return to the issue of justifying Kant's ethics on the basis of Levinas' existential grounding. Since Kierkegaard's "leap of faith" will do this for us, we can already note that the justification of Kantian ethics comes after the command of the face-to-face is waged and in the obedient response to this command. That is, Kantian theory is justified precisely at the moment when the call to responsibility is answered by *my* concrete moral response.

The justification of Kantian ethics by its existential grounding is deeply tied to what Kierkegaard calls the paradox of faith. This paradox has two components. It is "that the single individual as the single individual is higher than the universal" (*FT* 55) and that "the single individual as the single individual stands in an absolute relation to the absolute" (*FT* 56). The first component suggests that in the act of faith—the act of obedience to the divine command of the other—the individual who asserts his individuality, thereby falling out of the universal, does not sin. He is higher than the universal, and it is precisely his faith (obedience to God) that has made him that way. This theme is intimately tied to the second component of faith. That is, the single individual as the single individual is higher than the universal precisely because he is in absolute relation to the absolute. If the individual is in absolute relation to the absolute, he has no need of the mediation of the universal in his relation to the absolute. In being absolutely related to the absolute, the individual circumvents the universal, which is the expression of the absolute. Kierkegaard puts it this way: "The paradox of faith, then, is this: that the single individual is higher than the universal, that the single individual—to recall a distinction in dogmatics rather rare these days—determines his relation to the universal by his relation to the absolute, not his relation to the absolute by his relation to the universal" (*FT* 70).

In our present terminology, this means that the individual's relation to the universal ethics of Kant is determined on the basis of the existential condition of the face-to-face, and not the other way around. The moral law is not an intermediary between interpersonal relationship; rather, interpersonal relationship is the absolute that founds and sanctions the moral law. Here, my response to the other addresses the other directly and not through the intermediary of the law. But this very response also entails that I, as individual, become the single individual and the other, as concrete other, becomes singular as well. No longer are we dealing with the general "rational agents" of Kant's moral law. We have moved to the level of proper names.

The remarkable thing about my response is that in submitting to the other following Levinas' guidelines I am actually sanctioning the law. I *am* treating the other as an end-in-himself; so much so, that I am no longer confining him to the system of law, the universal as such. By the same token, the very same act singularizes the self and situates me beyond universal reason as well. Thus, in my concrete moral experience both self and other become ends-in-themselves. But this is precisely what the law demanded in the first place. This places us in the paradoxical situation of affirming the validity of the law by suspending it in order to carry it out.

We can make all of this explicit by taking a closer look at the categorical imperative in light of Levinas' conception of violence. To inscribe the other within reason violates the other by reducing the other to the self. Insofar as this inscription is a matter of using the other to satisfy my desire, my act of inscription means that I am using the other as a means to my own end. Since the categorical imperative entails that I must treat the other also as an end-in-herself, and since, for Levinas, this means that I treat her as an individual in the concrete situation of the face-to-face, I must resist the temptation to include her within the domain of universal reason. This is precisely the meaning of the injunction, "thou shall not kill." Furthermore, the same gesture that lets the other out of the universal individualizes the self, following Kierkegaard, since this response of obedience is *my* response. So, the very act of carrying out the categorical imperative means that the imperative is suspended. By acting out the precepts of the law, I affirm my singularity and the singularity of the other; both self and other are now situated outside of the universal order. Thus, in attempting to follow the categorical imperative concretized in the face-to-face, we have inadvertently violated it.

Such a gesture would place us in the grip of sin, if there were no "faith." If ethics did not emerge in the concrete situation of the face-to-face, then carrying out the law would be immoral. But Kierkegaard's paradox of faith allows for the universal, once again, to serve the individual without leading to sin. The paradox—that the single individual as the single individual is higher than the universal—means that in responding obediently to the other, the law is suspended. However, it is not "invalidated; rather, the ethical receives a completely different expression . . . " (*FT* 70).

The law is suspended, not annihilated, precisely because, after the momentary suspension of the law, the law is given back, redeemed. Once again, this can be made explicit in the language of the categorical imperative. If we must suspend the categorical imperative in order to fulfill it, that is, in order to treat the other as an end-in-itself, this means also that the very act of suspending the law affirms the validity of the law. After all, in suspending the law, we *are* treating the other as an end-in-itself; but this is precisely what the law demanded in the first place. So, we get the law back, but it is now justified by the immediacy of the face-to-face situation that ordered me to suspend it. It is justified because it situates the universal on the foundations of the concrete moment when the law is *handed down to me in particular*. In this way, Kantian ethics is justified by Levinas' existential foundations in every moment where the face of the other calls me immediately to action and I respond. Kierkegaard captures the same moment with regard to faith:

> Faith is precisely the paradox that the single individual as the single individual is higher than the universal, is justified before it, not as inferior to it but as superior—yet in such a way, please note, that it is the single individual who, after being subordinate as the single individual to the universal, now by means of the universal becomes the single individual who as the single individual is superior, that the single individual as the single individual stands in an absolute relation to the absolute. (*FT* 55-56)

Obedience to God, the absolute, is what justifies the law. In Levinas' terminology, obedience to the command of the other, that is, becoming responsible to and for the other, is what justifies the law. Without this responsibility, *my* responsibility, the law is simply an empty rational structure that violates the other and confines the self. My responsibility to the other is what makes the law refer to the other without including him in it. Thus, the system can only be justified on the basis of *my* personal responsibility to the concrete other.

Thus, in searching for the existential condition of moral experience, we have found a way to situate Levinas existentially "beneath" Kant's metaphysics of morals. What this means for us is that Kant's ethics can serve as a normative ethics on behalf of Levinas' grounding, but only when it is reined in by the individualizing nature of the face-to-face situation that makes responsibility uniquely *mine*. The directive that Levinas imposes on Kant's ethics to make it good is precisely that the law is moral only in becoming concrete, since only in the concrete does the moral law receive its ultimate sanction. But this means that responsibility can never be shared, that the social order can only be made moral on the basis of the individual responsibility of its citizens and not on the collective responsibility of it social institutions. I cannot pay the Internal Revenue Service to fulfill my social responsibility for me. *I* must feed the widow and the orphan, and welcome the stranger in my midst. Only by my doing can the said be unsaid.

Conclusions

In Chapter Two, I promised to explain the connection between self-esteem and generosity that Descartes left unclarified. Having shown the origins of responsibility in contact with the other and the existential conditions that surround the possibility of responding to the command of the other, we are now in a position to understand how generosity (deference to the other) might serve as an existential condition for self-esteem. Furthermore, understanding this integral connection will also clarify what the origins of responsible selfhood mean for the "scandal of philosophy" examined in Chapter One.

According to Descartes, true self-esteem is possible only when the will is committed to doing right. Since willed acts fall under the control of the individual self, these acts reflect back on the person. Thus, a person who wills to do what is right is worthy of self-esteem. This person is morally autonomous; he has a choice between a desire and an ought. Thus, he is free, and in being free he can be the recipient of praise or blame (esteem or contempt) for his actions.

When these observations are coupled with Levinas' analysis of the birth of the moral ought in the face-to-face situation, it becomes clear that the existential condition of self-esteem includes the face-to-face situation as well. For here, in the face-to-face, a desire is contested thereby opening up the divergence between want and ought necessary to make the individual morally free. Here, Levinas stops his analysis, focusing on the condition and birth of moral freedom and not on what the self does with this freedom. When we continue in a Levinasian style, and examine the moment of response existentially, it becomes clear that the very freedom of the individual to respond or not to respond means that the individual's choice reflects his goodness or badness. So, while the epiphany of the other gives the self its moral freedom precisely by endowing consciousness with an ought, the moment of response remains the self's deed. This allows the self who responds positively a justified claim to self-esteem.

More importantly the positive moral response to the other completes the self, because only in answering the call to responsibility does the self become justified as an independent self. This becomes clear when we bring Kierkegaard back into the picture. As I noted earlier, Levinas focuses on the birth of the moral ought by examining the other's resistance to the ego's possessive tendencies. Kierkegaard focuses on what happens after the command of the other; he focuses on the individual's response to the absolute. Between the two thinkers, however, we see an interesting dynamic: the other who comes from beyond the world, the system, also frees the self from the system. As I noted earlier, Levinas writes, "It is not I who resist the system, as Kierkegaard thought; it is the other" (*TI* 40). The other's resistance to the system is what animates the ethical in Levinas. That the command of the other comes from beyond the system is what makes the "absurd" absurd in Kierkegaard. But while the other's resistance to the system might characterize the moment that the ethical command is made, following Levinas, the possibility of my response—which individualizes me insofar as it is *my* deed— means that I fall out of the system as well, following Kierkegaard.

But this freedom from the system characterizes any individual posed between a desire and God's command, that is, any individual in Kierkegaard's "spiritual trial," since in his freedom he has become a single individual. But only the individual who responds positively to the other is justified in his singularity. Those who do not respond positively, sin. We find, then, two modes of individuality, one justified by obedience to moral authority, the other made sinful by a departure from the universal with no regard for the other. This means that the completely independent and autonomous self who is justified in being an individual (and, therefore, worthy of self-esteem) becomes a justified individual only because of his deference to the other.

This realization has another significance. If the other emerges from beyond the system and, therefore, opens up the moral freedom of the self, and if the self is now individualized because of this moral freedom, then the self is also situated beyond the system. Indeed, the very unforeseeability of the self, not only to the other, but also to the self, lends the self a noumenal, other-worldly character. But this free self is a soul in need of justification. She is fallen. When she responds positively to the command of the other—the will of God—she is justified. When she does not, she sins. The result is that when the self responds positively to the other, she too becomes like a god, sanctified and acceptable as a holy and moral individual, who is not of this world even though she is in it.[15]

The individual's positive moral response to the other means that both self and other meet beyond the world. If the world is the system, or the rational order, then we have found a means of escaping the confines of rational subjectivity discussed in Chapter One. When I turn my attention from reason to my concrete moral response by welcoming the other as stranger in my midst, I meet the other face-to-face. The "scandal of philosophy" is, therefore, as Heidegger suggested, that the question of the existence of the external world has been asked, but not because the rational world departs from the world of function, which is still a rational—albeit social—world. The question is a scandal because exteriority is given in the moment of face-to-face contact. The other is already indicated at the origin of the freedom and responsibility that defines the individualized self. Of course, none of this is apparent without obedient submission to the moral authority of the face. This is because the alternative to obedience is the violent gesture that kills the other.

If the self meets the other in the face-to-face, then the self, though independent and separated from the other, is not alone, provided that it does not kill the other. In turn, the self is not alone only by being responsible to the other. Furthermore, if the self is not alone, and if an object exists for both the self and the other, then the object exists apart from the self. This still does not allow us to claim that the object exists in its own right as a thing-in-itself; but it does mean that it exists beyond subjectivity in a realm that is truly intersubjective. This is the most that can be claimed for the external existence of objects in the world.

The world, existing "externally" in an intersubjective region, is the system; its status as external is given only in the realization that there are other subjects. This means that the world itself is situated on the relationship between self and other, which must be prior. Once we place the face-to-face situation at the origin of the world, we situate the system relative to the self and the other. The "scandal of philosophy" is that in making the system absolute, it has misunderstood its origins. The system originates from a prior foundation of sociality, revealed only in obedient submission to the other. It was made to serve sociality, not to replace it.

Originary sociality is interpersonal which, only later, converts into an order of social institutions. Thus, the preliminary meaning of "social" as interpersonal is extended to mean "social" as institutional, as when we speak of "social security" or the "socio-political" world. This means that the socio-political world is justified at its inception, and it remains so only to the extent that it respects its ethical origins and responds positively to the requirements of ethics which constitute its existential condition. Unfortunately, pursuing this theme further would carry us away from ethics and into politics. It should, therefore, be reserved for another volume.

NOTES

Abbreviations

BN	Sartre, *Being and Nothingness*
BT	Heidegger, *Being and Time*
CM	Husserl, *Cartesian Meditations*
CPR	Kant, *The Critique of Pure Reason*
EI	Levinas, *Ethics and Infinity*
FT	Kierkegaard, *Fear and Trembling*
GMM	Kant, *The Grounding for the Metaphysics of Morals*
Meta	Aristotle, *Metaphysics*
OBBE	Levinas, *Otherwise than Being*
PWD	Descartes, *The Philosophical Writings of Descartes*
TI	Levinas, *Totality and Infinity*
TIHP	Levinas, *The Theory of Intuition in Husserl's Phenomenology*

Introduction

1   Emmanuel Levinas, *Ethics and Infinity: Conversations with Philippe Nemo*, trans. Richard Cohen (Pittsburgh: Duquesne University Press, 1985), 60. Hereafter, *EI*. The first mention of a source will be documented in an endnote. Subsequent references will be documented internally.

2   Roland Paul Blum, "Emmanuel Levinas' Theory of Commitment," *Philosophy and Phenomenological Research* 44 (1983): 150.

Chapter One

1   All references to Descartes' work will be to *The Philosophical Writings of Descartes*, trans. and ed. John Cottingham, et. al., 3 vols. (Cambridge: Cambridge University Press, 1984-1991), unless otherwise noted. References to this text will be abbreviated as *PWD* followed by the volume number and page number. The current reference is *PWD* II 12.

2   Cottingham records that the phrase "and were independent of every other being" was added at this point in the French edition.

3   Immanuel Kant, *The Critique of Pure Reason*, trans. Norman Kemp Smith (New York: St. Martin's, 1965), 34. Hereafter, *CPR*.

4   Norman Kemp Smith, *A Commentary to Kant's* 'Critique of Pure Reason,' 2nd ed. (New York: Humanities, 1962), 220.

5   Robert Paul Wolff, *Kant's Theory of Mental Activity: A Commentary on the Transcendental Analytic of the* Critique of Pure Reason (Gloucester, MA: Peter Smith, 1973), 73. Hereafter, Wolff.

6   This point is made by Wolff: "Before we can analyze the representations of Socrates and Plato in order to abstract from them the concept of 'humanity,' we must first have held together in one consciousness the manifold of perceptions which each representation contains. The representation of Socrates, for example, contains the perceptions of his wit, his snub nose, his arms and legs and organs, the sharpness of his tongue, and so forth. If it were not for the fact that we had already thought of these perceptions as a unity, there would be no representation of Socrates to analyze. . . . Consequently, the mind must create them by a spontaneous act of unifying, an act to which Kant gives the title *synthesis*. The synthetic unity of a manifold of perceptions is thus the necessary condition of the analytic unity of a concept, and indeed of all knowledge and experience" (Wolff 68-69).

7   It is difficult to see what the "passive receptivity" that characterizes sensible intuition offers the understanding. Kant apparently underestimates passive receptivity, not finding in it anything that contributes to knowledge. His tendency to construe knowledge solely in terms of the activity of the ego is at the heart of his "Copernican Revolution," which has the net result of "making the realm of existing objects dependent upon the subjective conditions of knowledge" (Wolff 97).

8   Stephan Körner, *Kant* (New Haven, CT: Yale University Press, 1955), 94.

9   Edmund Husserl, *Ideas: General Introduction to Pure Phenomenology*, trans. W. R. Boyce Gibson (New York: Collier, 1962), 102-103.

10   Edmund Husserl, *Cartesian Meditations: An Introduction to Phenomenology*, trans. Dorion Cairns (Boston: Nijhoff, 1960), 25. Hereafter, *CM*.

11   As reported in Helmut R. Wagner, *Alfred Schutz: An Intellectual Biography* (Chicago: The University of Chicago Press, 1983), 311.

12   Emmanuel Levinas, *The Theory of Intuition in Husserl's Phenomenology*, trans. André Orianne (Evanston, IL: Northwestern University Press, 1973), 157. Hereafter, *TIHP*.

13   Martin Heidegger, *Being and Time*, trans. John Macquarrie and Edward Robinson (New York: Harper and Row, 1962), 68. Hereafter, *BT*.

14   Emmanuel Levinas, *Totality and Infinity: An Essay on Exteriority*, trans. Alphonso Lingis (Pittsburgh: Duquesne University Press, 1969), 133. Hereafter, *TI*.

Chapter Two

1   Further evidence for this position is given in the "Fourth Set of Replies": " . . . I do not think I proved too much in showing that the mind can exist apart from the body. Nor do I think I proved too little in saying that the mind is substantially united with the body, since that substantial union does not prevent our having a clear and distinct concept of the mind on its own, as a complete thing" (*PWD* II 160).

2   In the "Letter to the Sorbonne" Descartes writes, " . . . [A]lthough the proofs I
     employ here are in my view as certain and evident as the proofs of geometry, if
     not more so, it will, I fear, be impossible for many people to achieve an adequate
     perception of them, both because they are rather long and some depend on others,
     and also, above all, because they require a mind which is completely free from
     preconceived opinions and which can easily detach itself from involvement with
     the senses" (*PWD* II 5). In the "Preface to the reader," he writes, " . . . I do not
     expect any popular approval, or indeed any wide audience. On the contrary I
     would not urge anyone to read this book except those who are able and willing
     to meditate seriously with me, and to withdraw their minds from the senses and
     from all preconceived opinions" (*PWD* II 8).

3   If the method of withdrawing the mind from the senses is necessary for metaphys-
     ical inquiry, then Cartesian meditation must be thought of as a departure from
     embodied, practical life and an entry into another domain of existence. Further-
     more, mind-body dualism can no longer be thought of as an unwanted result of
     Cartesian meditation, but rather as a prerequisite for it.

4   Descartes notes the distinction between imagination and sensation in *The Conver-
     sation with Burman*: "When external objects act on my senses, they print on them
     an idea, or rather a figure, of themselves; and when the mind attends to these
     images imprinted on the gland in this way, it is said to have sensory perception.
     When, on the other hand, the images on the gland are not imprinted by external
     objects but by the mind itself, which fashions and shapes them in the brain in the
     absence of external objects, then we have imagination. The difference between
     sense-perception and imagination is thus really just this, that in sense-perception
     the images are imprinted by external objects which are actually present, whilst in
     imagination the images are imprinted by the mind without any external objects,
     and with the windows shut, as it were" (*PWD* III 344-345).

5   *Descartes: Philosophical Letters*, trans. and ed. Anthony Kenny (Minneapolis:
     University of Minnesota Press, 1970), 136.

6   In a letter to Regius, Descartes explains why he has focused his energies on prov-
     ing the distinction rather than the union between body and soul. " . . . [M]any
     more people make the mistake of thinking that the soul is not really distinct from
     the body than make the mistake of admitting their distinction and denying their
     substantial union . . . " (*PWD* III 209). It is interesting to note that the latter
     position, perhaps the position that might best be titled "Cartesian Dualism," is
     termed a "mistake." Descartes departs from this position because he thinks that
     while mind and body are really distinct, they are also substantially unified, though
     they cannot be understood to be so within the parameters of what he calls the
     "pure intellect."

7   Descartes begins the second letter, "I am very obliged to Your Highness because
     although she saw how badly I explained myself in my last letter about the ques-
     tion she was good enough to put to me, she still has enough patience to listen to
     me on the same subject and to give me the opportunity to mention the things I left
     out" (*PWD* III 226). Thus, the two letters form a topical unit, though the second

is corrective of the first and provides more detail of the theory needed to answer the question. For this reason, I will treat the two letters together, preferring the details of the second letter to the first where the two diverge.

8   Further, evidence for this claim is seen in the sarcastic humor that motivates Descartes' replies to Gassendi: " . . . you address me no longer as a whole man but as a disembodied soul. I think that you are indicating here that these objections of yours did not originate in the mind of a subtle philosopher but came from flesh alone. I ask you then, O Flesh, or whatever name you want me to address you by, have you so little to do with the mind that you were unable to notice . . . " (*PWD* II 244). Throughout this set of objections and replies Descartes and Gassendi refer to each other as Mind and Flesh, respectively.

9   Maurice Merleau-Ponty, "Eye and Mind," trans. Carleton Dallery, in *The Primacy of Perception and Other Essays on Phenomenological Psychology, the Philosophy of Art, History and Politics,* ed. James M. Edie (Evanston, IL: Northwestern University Press, 1964), 176.

10   Jean-Luc Marion, "Generosity and Phenomenology: Remarks on Michel Henry's Interpretation of the Cartesian *Cogito*," trans. Stephen Voss, in *Essays on the Philosophy and Science of René Descartes*, ed. Stephen Voss (Oxford: Oxford University Press, 1993), 66.

11   In several places, Descartes suggests that the ability to withdraw the mind from the senses is easier for someone who is older and physically healthy. For instance, he writes to Hyperaspistes, "We know by experience that our minds are so closely joined to our bodies as to be almost always acted upon by them; and although when thriving in an adult and healthy body the mind enjoys some liberty to think of other things than those presented by the senses, we know there is not the same liberty in those who are sick or asleep or very young; and the younger they are, the less liberty they have" (*PWD* III 189-190). It would be interesting to explore the process of withdrawal as a consequence of maturation, but this issue lies beyond the scope of the current work.

12   Descartes writes, " . . . [A]ll the animals devoid of reason conduct their lives simply through bodily movements similar to those which, in our case, usually follow upon the passions which move our soul to consent to such movements. Nevertheless it is not always good for the passions to function in this way, in so far as there are many things harmful to the body which cause no sadness initially (or which even produce joy), and in so far as other things are useful to the body, although at first they are disagreeable" (*PWD* I 376-377).

Chapter Three

1   Lingis writes, "In *Totality and Infinity* the relationship with the other [person] was presented as a contestation of the pure sensibility, in which the ego pursues its own closure and contentment. Now Levinas actually sets out to see in the exposedness to alterity in the face of another the original form of openness. It even founds and sustains the openness to things . . . " The translator's introduction to

Emmanuel Levinas, *Otherwise than Being or Beyond Essence,* trans. Alphonso Lingis (Boston: Nijhoff, 1981), xvi. Hereafter, *OBBE.*

2   Aristotle, *Metaphysics,* trans. W. D. Ross, in *The Basic Works of Aristotle,* ed. Richard McKeon (New York: Random House, 1941), 689. Hereafter, *Meta.*

3   This point is made over and over again in the *Cartesian Meditations.* See, for instance, *CM* 42: "The 'object' of consciousness, the object as having identity 'with itself' during the flowing subjective process, does not come into the process from outside; on the contrary, it is included as a sense in the subjective process itself—and is thus as an '*intentional effect*' *produced by* the synthesis of consciousness."

4   This is at the root of Levinas' criticism of Husserl: "[t]he Husserlian thesis of the primacy of the objectifying act—in which was seen Husserl's excessive attachment to theoretical consciousness, and which has served as a pretext to accuse Husserl of intellectualism . . . leads to transcendental philosophy, to the affirmation . . . that the object of consciousness, while distinct from consciousness, is as it were a product of consciousness, being a "meaning" endowed by consciousness . . . " (*TI* 123).

5   Levinas envisions the entire history of Western Philosophy as a conceptual endeavor that overplays the use of representations. Concerning this history, he writes: "[The history of philosophy] can be interpreted as an attempt at universal synthesis, a reduction of all experience, of all that is reasonable, to a totality wherein consciousness embraces the world, leaves nothing other outside of itself, and thus becomes absolute thought. The consciousness of self is at the same time the consciousness of the whole" (*EI* 75). Taking this claim seriously, it would seem that the phenomenological reduction is a world-class event occurring within human history. It would be interesting to explore world history as the internalization of consciousness and eclipse of the other, thereby historicizing Levinas as Hegel did Kant. Levinas almost undertakes this analysis himself, though he never presents it systematically. No doubt, such an investigation would provide a fruitful analysis of Western history. I plan to take it up in later research.

6   See Emmanuel Levinas, "On the Trial of the Other," *Philosophy Today,* 10 (1966): 43. "Have we been faithful enough to the injunction against looking for the *beyond* as a world behind our world? The order of being will thus be again supposed, an order which does not permit any other status than that of revealed or dissimulated. In Being, a transcendence revealed, is inverted into immanence, the extra-ordinary inserts itself into an order, the other is absorbed into the Same."

7   See Steven G. Smith, "Reason as One for Another: Moral and Theoretical Argument in the Philosophy of Levinas," *Journal of the British Society for Phenomenology* 12 (1981): 231-232. "According to Levinas, the Western philosophical tradition is overwhelmingly devoted to the problem of theoretical truth. Its approach may be epistemological, i.e. attentive to the necessary structure of knowing, or ontological, i.e. attentive to the necessary structure of being; but there is a root complicity between the two emphases. It is the destiny of knowledge to

search out and adhere to being, and it is the destiny of being to disclose itself to be known. The bias towards the "theoretical," in this inclusive sense, unites such diverse thinkers as Husserl and Heidegger. [But] *Totality and Infinity*'s main thesis is that justice is prior to truth." The priority of justice over truth, as we shall see, is also the priority of metaphysics over both epistemology and ontology.

8   Richard A. Cohen, "Emmanuel Levinas: Happiness is a Sensational Time," *Philosophy Today* 25 (1981): 197. Hereafter, Cohen.

9   Craig R. Vasey, "Emmanuel Levinas: From Intentionality to Proximity," *Philosophy Today* 25 (1981): 182.

10   John Patrick Burke, "The Ethical Significance of the Face," *ACPA Proceedings* 56 (1982): 198. Hereafter, Burke.

11   See *OBBE* 5: "Saying is not a game. Antecedent to the verbal signs it conjugates, to the linguistic systems and the semantic glimmerings, a foreword preceding languages, it is the proximity of one to the other, the commitment of an approach, the one for the other, the very signifyingness of signification."

12   See Robert Bernasconi, "Levinas Face to Face—With Hegel," *Journal of the British Society for Phenomenology* 13 (1982): 273. "The Other overflows me as an excess so that I cannot contain him or her, the face, the infinity."

13   Note the Jewish element at play here. See Rudolph J. Gerber, "Totality and Infinity: Hebraism & Hellenism—The Experiential Ontology of Emmanuel Levinas," *Review of Existential Psychology & Psychiatry* 7 (1967): 183. "For the Hebraic mind, transcendence accomplishes an exterior movement towards the other which severs self-totality and all the while respects the identity of the self and the alterity of the other. The other is not reducible to the self nor is the self reducible to the other: Both are confirmed rather than destroyed in their very separation."

Chapter Four

1   Andrius Valevicius, *From the Other to the Totally Other: The Religious Philosophy of Emmanuel Levinas* (New York: Peter Lang, 1988), 89.

2   Jacques Derrida, "Violence and Metaphysics," in *Writing and Difference*, 79-153, trans. Alan Bass (Chicago: The University of Chicago Press, 1978), 128.

3   Robert R. Ehman, "Emmanuel Levinas: The Phenomenon of the Other," *Man and World* 8 (1975): 144. It seems to me that Ehman has set up a false dichotomy here. Levinas does not maintain that I give everything to the other, but that I owe him a justification for my not doing so. His point is that I am accountable to the other.

4   Immanuel Kant, *Grounding for the Metaphysics of Morals*, trans. James W. Ellington (Indianapolis: Hackett, 1981), 36. Hereafter, *GMM*.

5   Robert Dennis Walsh, *The Priority of Responsibility in the Ethical Philosophy of Emmanuel Levinas* (Milwaukee: Marquette University, Unpublished Dissertation, 1989), 271.

6   The look is multidimensional. It indicates not only that the other is other, but it also reveals my being-for-others. See Jean-Paul Sartre, *Being and Nothingness: A Phenomenological Essay on Ontology*, trans. Hazel E. Barnes (New York: Washington Square, 1956), 475. Hereafter, *BN*. "If we start with the first revelation of the Other as a *look*, we must recognize that we experience our inapprehensible being-for-others in the form of a *possession*. I am possessed by the Other; the Other's look fashions my body in its nakedness, causes it to be born, sculptures it, produces it as it is, sees it as I shall never see it."

7   Jean-Paul Sartre, *Baudelaire*, trans. Martin Turnell (New York: New Directions, 1950), 52.

8   Truman Capote, *In Cold Blood: A True Account of a Multiple Murder and Its Consequences* (New York: Signet, 1965). Hereafter, Capote.

9   Richard Eugene Hickock, "America's Worst Crime in Twenty Years," in *Truman Copote's* In Cold Blood: *A Critical Handbook*, ed. Irving Malin (Belmont, CA: Wadsworth, 1968), 10. Hereafter, Hickock.

10   Descartes writes, " . . . I believe that true generosity, which causes a person's self-esteem to be as great as it may legitimately be, has only two components. The first consists in his knowing that nothing truly belongs to him but this freedom to dispose his volitions, and that he ought to be praised or blamed for no other reason than his using this freedom well or badly. The second consists in his feeling within himself a firm and constant resolution to use it well—that is, never to lack the will to undertake and carry out whatever he judges to be best. To do that is to pursue virtue in a perfect manner" (*PWD* I 384). When Descartes notes that generosity consists in "using the will well" and in a "firm and constant resolution to use it well," he is setting up the conditions for moral autonomy. This situation was examined back Chapter Two.

11   Emmanuel Levinas, *Nine Talmudic Readings*, trans. Annette Aronowicz (Bloomington, IN: Indiana University Press, 1990), 166.

12   This condition is documented in the Genesis myth of Adam and Eve. Here, Adam and Eve are set up to choose between their desire and God's command, which is strictly opposed to this desire. Thus, the story documents the birth of moral freedom and responsibility as human independence from God, that is, moral subjectivity. The story, therefore, continues the creation of the human being that is begun in the previous chapter. I am currently working on a paper that examines this story in this light.

13   Following the line of reasoning that characterizes the current chapter, we have found an existential connection between rights and responsibilities that underlies Kant's abstract connection. Exploring this further would carry us slightly beyond

the scope of the current work. I intend to examine this connection more closely in future work.

14   Søren Kierkegaard, *Fear and Trembling: Repetition*, trans. Howard V. Hong and Edna H. Hong (Princeton: Princeton University Press, 1983), 56. Hereafter, *FT*.

15   The inversion that allows an individual to live in the world without being of it follows from a broader transition that is hiding in the background. This is the transition from the Jewish concept of God as absolute other to the Christian concept of the incarnate Christ. The incarnation of the absolute other in the person of Christ "fulfills the law" without overturning it. I am currently in the process of examining what happens to Levinas' ethical structures as a result of this transition. I believe that this research will eventually offer an explanation of the Judeo-Christian tradition in its historical, spiritual, ethical and political contexts, thereby opening up the possibility of a rather rich Christian theology.

Works Cited

Aristotle. *Metaphysics*. Trans. W. D. Ross. In *The Basic Works of Aristotle*, ed. Richard McKeon, 681-926. New York: Random House, 1941.

Bernasconi, Robert. "Levinas Face to Face—With Hegel." *Journal of the British Society for Phenomenology* 13 (1982): 267-276.

Blum, Roland Paul. "Emmanuel Levinas' Theory of Commitment." *Philosophy and Phenomenological Research* 44 (1983): 145-168.

Burke, John Patrick. "The Ethical Significance of the Face." *ACPA Proceedings* 56 (1982): 194-206.

Cohen, Richard A. "Emmanuel Levinas: Happiness is a Sensational Time." *Philosophy Today* 25 (1981): 196-203.

Capote, Truman. *In Cold Blood: A True Account of a Multiple Murder and Its Consequences*. New York: Signet, 1965.

Derrida, Jacques. "Violence and Metaphysics." In *Writing and Difference*, trans. Alan Bass, 79-153. Chicago: The University of Chicago Press, 1978.

Descartes, René. *Descartes: Philosophical Letters*. Trans. and ed. Anthony Kenny. Minneapolis: The University of Minnesota Press, 1970.

_____. *The Philosophical Writings of Descartes*. Trans. and ed. John Cottingham, et. al. 3 Vols. Cambridge: Cambridge University Press, 1984-1991.

Ehman, Robert R. "Emmanuel Levinas: The Phenomenon of the Other." *Man and World* 8 (1975): 141-145.

Gerber, Rudolph J. "Totality and Infinity: Hebraism & Hellenism—The Experiential Ontology of Emmanuel Levinas." *Review of Existential Psychology & Psychiatry* 7 (1967): 177-188.

Heidegger, Martin. *Being and Time*. Trans. John Macquarrie and Edward Robinson. New York: Harper & Row, 1962.

Hickock, Richard Eugene. "America's Worst Crime in Twenty Years." In *Truman Capote's* In Cold Blood: *A Critical Handbook*, ed. Irving Malin, 8-24. Belmont, CA: Wadsworth, 1968.

Husserl, Edmund. *Cartesian Meditations: An Introduction to Phenomenology*. Trans. Dorion Cairns. Boston: Nijhoff, 1960.

_____. *Ideas: General Introduction to Pure Phenomenology*. Trans. W. R. Boyce Gibson. New York: Collier, 1962.

Kant, Immanuel. *The Critique of Pure Reason*. Trans. Norman Kemp Smith. New York: St. Martin's, 1965.

_____. *Grounding for the Metaphysics of Morals*. Trans. James W. Ellington. Indianapolis: Hackett, 1981.

Kemp Smith, Norman. *A Commentary to Kant's* 'Critique of Pure Reason. 2nd ed. New York: Humanities, 1962.

Kierkegaard, Søren. *Fear and Trembling: Repetition*. Trans. Howard V. Hong and Edna H. Hong. Princeton: Princeton University Press, 1983.

Körner, Stephan. *Kant*. New Haven, CT: Yale University Press, 1955.

Levinas, Emmanuel. *Ethics and Infinity: Conversations with Philippe Nemo*. Trans. Richard A. Cohen. Pittsburgh: Duquesne University Press, 1985.

_____. *Nine Talmudic Readings*. Trans. Annette Aronowicz. Bloomington, IN: Indiana University Press, 1990.

_____. "On the Trial of the Other." *Philosophy Today* 10 (1966): 34-46.

_____. *Otherwise than Being or Beyond Essence*. Trans. Alphonso Lingis. Boston: Nijhoff, 1981.

_____. *The Theory of Intuition in Husserl's Phenomenology*. Trans. André Orianne. Evanston, IL: Northwestern University Press, 1973.

_____. *Totality and Infinity: An Essay on Exteriority*. Trans. Alphonso Lingis. Pittsburgh: Duquesne University Press, 1969.

Marion, Jean-Luc. "Generosity and Phenomenology: Remarks on Michel Henry's Interpretation of the Cartesian *Cogito*." Trans. Stephen Voss. In *Essays on the Philosophy and Science of René Descartes*, ed. Stephen Voss, 52-74. Oxford: Oxford University Press, 1993.

Merleau-Ponty, Maurice. "Eye and Mind." Trans. Carleton Dallery. In *The Primacy of Perception and Other Essays on Phenomenological Psychology, the Philosophy of Art, History and Politics*, ed. James M. Edie, 159-190. Evanston, IL: Northwestern University Press, 1964.

Sartre, Jean-Paul. *Baudelaire*. Trans. Martin Turnell. New York: New Directions, 1950.

_____. *Being and Nothingness: A Phenomenological Essay on Ontology*. Trans. Hazal E. Barnes. New York: Washington Square, 1956.

Smith, Steven G. "Reason as One for Another: Moral and Theoretical Argument in the Philosophy of Levinas." *Journal of the British Society for Phenomenology* 12 (1981): 231-244.

Valevicius, Andrius. *From the Other to the Totally Other: The Religious Philosophy of Emmanuel Levinas*. New York: Peter Lang, 1988.

Vasey, Craig R. "Emmanuel Levinas: From Intentionality to Proximity." *Philosophy Today* 25 (1981): 178-195.

Wagner, Helmut R. *Alfred Schutz: An Intellectual Biography*. Chicago: The University of Chicago Press, 1983.

Walsh, Robert Dennis. *The Priority of Responsibility in the Ethical Philosophy of Emmanuel Levinas*. Milwaukee: Marquette University, Unpublished Dissertation, 1989.

Wolff, Robert Paul. *Kant's Theory of Mental Activity: A Commentary on the Transcendental Analytic of the* Critique of Pure Reason. Gloucester, MA: Peter Smith, 1973.